HOW TO UNDERSTAND YOUR DREAMS

by
Geoffrey A. Dudley, B.A.

Foreword by Melvin Powers

Published by
Melvin Powers
WILSHIRE BOOK COMPANY
12015 Sherman Road
No. Hollywood, California 91605
Telephone: (213) 875-1711

Printed by

HAL LEIGHTON PRINTING COMPANY
P.O. Box 3952
North Hollywood, California 91605
Telephone: (213) 983-1105

CONTENTS

ACKNOWLEDGMENTS

For permission to use quotations the author is indebted to George Allen & Unwin Ltd., publishers of *The Interpretation of Dreams* and *Introductory Lectures on Psycho-Analysis* by Sigmund Freud, *Adler's Place in Psychology* by Lewis Way, *The Mystery of Dreams* by William Oliver Stevens, and *Abnormal Psychology* by D. B. Klein; to the Hogarth Press Ltd., publishers of *New Introductory Lectures on Psycho-Analysis, On Dreams* and *An Autobiographical Study* by Sigmund Freud, and *Essays in Applied Psycho-Analysis* by Ernest Jones; to Victor Gollancz Ltd., publishers of *The Forgotten Language* by Erich Fromm; to Methuen & Co. Ltd., publishers of *Contemporary Schools of Psychology* by Robert S. Woodworth; to Rider and Company, publishers of *Autobiography of a Yogi* by Paramhansa Yogananda; to the Clarendon Press, publishers of Plato's *Phaedo* translated by B. Jowett; to Enid Blyton and Sampson Low, Marston & Co. Ltd., publishers of "I Certainly Didn't" in *The Sixth Holiday Book* by Enid Blyton; to the Editors of *Psychology*, the *Daily Express* and the *Sunday Dispatch*; and to Mrs M. Walls. The feature discussed in chapter XVIII was published in the Doctor's Diary of *Woman's Own* on September 20th, 1951, and is reproduced by courtesy of the Editor.

"If we relearn the mental language of our childhood, we can grasp the psychological meaning of our dreams."

—DR FRANZ ALEXANDER

FOREWORD

There are few books in literature that can introduce a new reader to the subject of understanding dreams without utterly confusing him. However, *How To Understand Your Dreams* has been so interestingly written that any layman can understand and beneficially apply its teachings to himself with little difficulty.

The first principle of dreams is that they are sheer creations of the mind, but not the conscious mind. It is the subconscious mind that fabricates dreams while the conscious mind sleeps. It uses the only language it has, a "primordial language" expressive of man and his forebears in a far earlier stage of evolution. This primordial language uses concrete, not abstract terms. For example, you can dream you are powerless, only by dreaming you are physically rigid and incapable of movement. Something dishonest will be expressed by an object actually crooked. You will dream of choosing something by physically picking it up. Using such concrete instances and images was the only way in which man's primitive mind could express abstract ideas. For this reason the primordial language of dreams must be translated back into civilized language. When you learn to do this, your dreams begin to take on meaning, and dream-analysis becomes a fascinating study.

For you to analyze your dreams, you must first remember them—and this is admittedly difficult. Since everyone dreams, you must begin by granting this. Next, you must perfect your technique for recapturing dreams. No matter how hopeless this may seem at first, it can be done. This is the procedure: When you awake in the morning, lie there a few minutes and recall everything possible about that night's dreams. Do not be discouraged if nothing can be remembered, for the habit of "recall" must be formed. This should take only a few days. At first you will only be able to catch the "tail-end" of a dream, so to speak, and drag this small part back into your memory. As you progress, more and more of a dream will be recaptured until several entire dreams a night can be recovered without difficulty.

The second step is to write down the dreams and their fragments. Do not become discouraged at this point if you think you are going too slow. The entire process becomes easier with time.

The third step is to see if the dreams form a pattern. If you have read and thoroughly digested this book, you will know what to look for. For instance, are there apparent instances of symbolism? Ambivalence? A death-wish? Everything learned in this book should be applied to yourself, and the best way to begin self-analysis is simply to begin it.

The most important thing to look for in your dream is its "primary effect," or the way it makes you feel. The mood should be identified, set down, and described unerringly. What was the dream's main emotion? Was it terror, wonder, horror, triumph? Do not be misled if the emotion in your dream is misplaced. Often an emotion does not occur in that part where it should, but is found attached to a foreign part of the dream. There are reasons for these displacements. Your main purpose now is to develop skill in finding and characterizing this primary effect.

With practice, it is possible for you to train yourself to analyze your own dreams in order to discover your "life conflict," the pattern of your present existence. Few discoveries could be of greater value than this.

Armed with the above ideas, and the firm resolution to put them into effect, *How To Understand Your Dreams* can be the first step toward that self-knowledge which men have admired and strived for since the dawn of general intelligence.

Melvin Powers

12015 Sherman Road
No. Hollywood, California 91605

Introduction

THE popular idea of a psychologist is of someone who can take one look at a person and instantly read his innermost soul. He is supposed to be able to unravel deeply buried complexes in the course of a five-minute interview, and tell a person what his intelligence quotient is after asking him a few simple questions. There are no secrets that are hidden from him and everybody's mind is an open book to him. He has a solution for every human problem and can hypnotize people with a mere wave of his hand.

Needless to say, this picture of the psychologist, like the reports of Mark Twain's death, is greatly exaggerated. We have to blame the films in part for the spread of this belief. There was a time when no film was complete without its psychiatrist or psychologist. Happily that era is passing to be replaced by a more balanced view of what psychology is capable of doing. The reader who picks up this book is urged to disabuse his mind of any false ideas that Hollywood may have implanted in it. The psychologist is not the man that the films would have us believe he is. He is just as much in the dark about some aspects of human nature as is the average man or woman.

Provided the reader does not expect too much of it, therefore, this is a book that will teach him something about his dreams. The subject is not an easy one to deal with, but there are several reasons why it merits the popular treatment that this book attempts to give it. In the first place, it is a subject that most psychologists have neglected, and so its novelty may appeal to the reader. Again, dreams in either their waking or sleeping form are phenomena of which most people have at least some first-hand experience. And further, dreams are so generally misunderstood that it may be useful to have the light of psychological ideas thrown on them. The essentials of Freud's theory of dreams, first put forward in 1900, still remain to be generally known.

The psychology of dreams cannot invariably be a pleasant topic for a reason which is inherent in the nature of dreams themselves.

It compels us to take notice of things that we would perhaps prefer to think did not exist at all. This is said by way of introduction in order to justify the need to remark upon certain matters that the reader may experience as distasteful.

"The apparently innocent dreams," points out Freud in *The Interpretation of Dreams*, "turn out to be quite the reverse when we take the trouble to analyse them. They are, if I may say so, wolves in sheep's clothing." It is often a difficult and delicate matter to convince a dreamer of the truth of this statement. He is apt to react with shock and disgust when his attention is called to these matters in spite of the fact that they occur in his own mental productions.

In putting this book into the hands of those to whom it is likely to appeal, however, the writer feels confident that for the most part anything that he says on these lines will be considered on a rational rather than an emotional level. The reader's reaction may be one of scepticism, but at least one hopes that he will not be shocked too profoundly. This will come about, no doubt, through his appreciation of the fact that nothing could be more natural than that sleep should provide us with a substitute outlet for those desires which in our waking life civilization may have compelled us to repress.

At this point one is faced with two alternative methods of approach to the subject. One can either start with explanations and bring in examples of actual dreams to illustrate them. That is what might be called the indirect method. The alternative is to deal with the actual dreams themselves, and analyse them with a view to discovering what we can learn from them.

After much debating with himself the author finally came to the conclusion that his purpose could best be served by a combination of both methods. The emphasis throughout, however, tends to fall on the direct method, which deals first with dreams and secondly with explanations. He therefore proposes to adopt this method in the hope that it will meet with the reader's approval and possibly prove the more interesting by combining the advantages of the two alternatives.

HOW TO READ THIS BOOK

There are two ways of reading a book of this kind. It can be read for its intellectual interest and educational value. The person who wishes to be thought well-informed cannot afford to neglect this important field of human behaviour and experience. It is up to him to make the knowledge that psychology has revealed a part of a well-stocked brain.

This does not, however, ensure that the person who picks up a book on psychology and reads through it will be better and happier when he puts it down. If the study that he has undertaken is to be of any real value to him, he must be prepared to let it make its own disturbing impact upon his preconceived notions and emotional prejudices. Only in this way will it bring about some abiding change in his mental outlook and attitude towards life.

That is why the second way of reading a book such as this is even more important. This second way is that the reader uses what he studies as a means of learning something about himself that he did not know before. If he is to get the full benefit from this book, he should let it stimulate the process of self-analysis. As he reads it, he will come upon something that seems to apply particularly to himself. This piece of knowledge may make him feel un-comfortable; it may bring back a flood of unpleasant memories, or make him see something that he had previously not understood.

At that point one should put the book down and let the mind dwell on what has been read, trying to make the experience a per-manent part of oneself. In some small way one will have been changed for the better. One will be able to claim a larger measure of the valuable quality of insight. The method may at times seem to strike one as being rather slow and haphazard, but it is the only way of reading books on psychology that makes a vital difference to one's life.

Sometimes the first sign that a book is making an abiding impression upon the reader is the fact that he tends to lose interest in it. He may reach a point where he begins to find it dull and tedious. This may throw some light on what is happening if you experience a wish to cast this book aside in favour of a light novel that does not ask you to think very deeply. If you seem to prefer something else that does not delve quite so deeply into human motives, it may mean that you have just read in these pages something that has a significant bearing on your life. Hitherto you may for some reason have been unwilling or unable to recognize it.

If you pause and ask yourself, "What has made me lose interest at this point?" you may be able to advance a further step along the road to self-knowledge.

With these words of advice and warning we wish you success on your journey of discovery into the land of dreams.

CHAPTER I

Plumbing the Depths of the Mind

ONE of the basic teachings of modern psychology is that there is a vast region of the mind which lies below the level of the ordinary waking conscious mind.

This means that there are mental processes which go on in us without our being aware of them. Outside our conscious thoughts and experiences lies a realm of mental life of whose existence we are normally ignorant. To these unknown mental processes we give the name of the unconscious.

Some readers will ask at this point: "Why do you use this term?" Such readers will be accustomed to refer to *subjective* and *subconscious* mental processes. They will find it hard to understand the need of the new term that we have employed above.

It is really not so hard to understand. When we separate and label mental processes that are not conscious, we do so in order to make it convenient for us to describe them. In reality, however, they are not separated. Since in this book we wish to consider subjective and subconscious processes together, we group them under the name of the unconscious.

The reader may assume, therefore, that when we refer to the unconscious, we include both subjective and subconscious mental processes. Some readers have a totally false idea of what the unconscious is like because they identify it only with the subconscious mind. They regard it as a wise but stern, kind but just, father upon whom they can call when things go wrong but whom they can ignore when things go right. Needless to say, the number of times that we deliberately influence our unconscious is few compared with the number of times that our unconscious spontaneously influences us.

Our waking thoughts and actions are constantly under the control of mental processes the nature of which is quite unknown to us. It is equally true, of course, that mental processes of whose existence we are fully aware can become unconscious, *i.e.*, we can direct the influence of the unconscious to our advantage.

PANDORA'S BOX

The discovery that this realm of mind exists is not new. What is new is the name that we give to it. Its existence was certainly known in ancient times, as indeed were other facts and principles which modern psychology has merely rediscovered. Of course, this knowledge was current then under a different name. Instead of referring to the unconscious the ancient world spoke of Pandora's box.

According to this legend, the god Mercury left a box in the care of Pandora with the warning that she should not open it. Her curiosity getting the better of her, she opened the box and allowed all the evils and sufferings of the world to escape.

This is simply a statement in mythological terms of the psychological truth that havoc would be wreaked if the forces of the unconscious were given free expression.

There is another side, however, to the unconscious. Pandora's box also contained the spirit of hope, which sustains and uplifts weary mankind. The unconscious is a repository of individual and racial wisdom. "Anything which we have ever known or read or seen or heard," write two modern authorities, "can, in certain circumstances, be dug up and brought out of the limbo of unconsciousness." That the ancient Greeks were aware of this, too, may be seen from their legend. (The name Pandora means "all gifts".)

"If we are unaware of the activity of the unconscious," the reader may ask, "how do we know that it exists at all?" This is a legitimate question which we must not attempt to evade. At first sight it does seem strange that we should know of the existence of something of which we are unaware. How can we explain this paradox?

The answer to the riddle is that we can explain certain features of mental life better if we assume that the unconscious exists than if we do not assume that it exists. To some psychologists this may seem too conservative a statement of the position. But our aim here is merely to stimulate thought and further enquiry, so we can afford to dispense with being dogmatic.

What are the features of mental life which require us to presume the working of unconscious mental processes in order to explain

2

them properly ? Sometimes we try to recall a name but fail to do so. Then we forget about the matter and later, when we are not thinking of it, the forgotten name springs to mind. A name which cannot be recalled at will but which springs to the conscious level unaided must have been at another level of mind. It was there but we did not know it. It was unconscious.

It can even happen that one arrives in this way at the solution of some difficult intellectual problem which has previously baffled one's efforts to solve it consciously.

SLIP OF THE TONGUE

Another experience that we can explain better if we assume that the unconscious exists is the performance of a faulty mental act—the making of an error of commission or omission. For example, called to the telephone one morning, I greeted the person at the other end with "Good afternoon". Subsequent reflection convinced me that, not feeling quite up to the mark but having a lot of work to do, I had suppressed the wish that the day might pass quickly. The thought, "I wish it were afternoon instead of morning," existed in me without my being aware of it at the time of the telephone call. It was this unconscious thought that was responsible for the mistake made while speaking on the phone. The wish that had been suppressed and made unconscious reasserted itself in the form of the mistaken greeting.

If it were possible to explain every other instance of a slip of the tongue in the same way, and similarly every slip of the pen, every case of misreading or mishearing, and every faulty action, it would really no longer be possible to dispute the fact that mental acts which are unconscious do exist and that they can sometimes get the better of conscious intentions.

Thirdly, we will refer to superstitions, which are a rich source of evidence for the existence of the unconscious. The essence of superstition is that we carry out some trivial act, *e.g.*, touching wood, throwing a pinch of spilt salt over our left shoulder, etc.

3

without knowing why we do it. The power of superstition is not diminished by intelligence. Even intelligent people will superstitiously refuse to hang up a new calendar before new-year's day on the grounds that it is "unlucky" to do so.

The widespread persistence of superstitions is proof that there must be powerful reasons for observing them, even though we do not know what these reasons are. The undue significance that attaches to them is due to the associations that exist between them and important thoughts and wishes of which we are unaware. Superstitions have a hidden logical meaning that reveals the working of unconscious mental processes. If we could gain insight into their meaning, *i.e.*, by becoming conscious of what was previously unconscious, superstitions would lose their hold over us.

The evidence for the existence of the unconscious derived from these three sources is too important to be lightly set on one side. Moreover, it is but a fraction of the vast body of evidence that might be brought forward from many other sources if space permitted. What has been said above, however, should suffice to prove the point without unduly trying the reader's patience with lengthy details.

CHAPTER II

What the Unconscious is like

THE reader who has patiently followed this argument so far may be inclined to say: "We will grant your point that the unconscious exists. But can you tell us what the unconscious is like?"

Let us see, then, what we can learn about the nature of the unconscious mind from a further study of some of the effects which it produces. If we expect to find that the unconscious mind is totally unlike anything that we know about the conscious mind, we shall probably not be disappointed.

If I were to ask you to describe a table, you would probably say that it was flat, smooth, square, brown, that it had four legs and was made of wood. I would accept your description as valid, because I concede to you the right to describe a table by listing those qualities which distinguish it from other objects. So you must concede to me the right to describe the unconscious mind by listing those qualities which distinguish it from the conscious mind. The list which I give you will not be complete, but at least it will convey some idea of what the unconscious mind is like.

(1) The first thing we learn is that opposite ideas exist side by side in the unconscious without contradicting each other. Traces of this survive in the language that we use in our everyday conscious lives. For example, the word "cleave" has two opposite meanings. It means not only "adhere" but also "separate".

This tendency may be observed even more distinctly in dreams, which are also products of the unconscious or dream-mind. A woman whose name was Maria dreamed that she carried a spray of flowers, such as the angel is represented as holding in pictures of the Annunciation. The flowers, however, were camellias, which the dreamer associated with the fallen woman in *La Dame aux Camélias*, a novel and play by the younger Alexandre Dumas. In other words, the unconscious symbol of the spray of flowers represented both purity and its opposite, because these conflicting ideas existed side by side in the woman's unconscious mind.

5

An element in a dream which admits of an opposite may stand for itself, for its opposite, or for both together.

Love and hatred also exist side by side in the unconscious, and it is very common to find an individual manifesting both at different times towards the same person. It is, of course, even commoner to find him manifesting both at the same time towards different persons, *e.g.*, he may love his mother and hate his father.

Here is an example of the less common manifestation of love and hatred by a person towards the same individual. "We were very affectionate towards each other," stated a young woman, referring to her brother, "but often quarrelled violently." Another young woman admitted that she lost her temper only with people who meant the most to her. "The person I have hurt most of all," she added, "is my mother, and yet she is everything in the world to me." A young man could not speak well enough of a girl— behind her back; yet when he met her face to face he insulted her.

OMNIPOTENCE OF THOUGHT

(2) Another characteristic of the unconscious is that it draws no distinction between thoughts and deeds. If a thing is wished unconsciously, the individual may act as though the wish had already been granted. The unconscious treats thoughts as omnipotent; in his unconscious a person has only to wish a thing for it to be so.

This feature is often seen in fairy-tales, which like dreams reflect unconscious wishes. For example, in the Grimms' fairy-tale, *The Wishing Table*, a feast appears on the magic table whenever its owner expresses a wish for it. The well-known play, *The Monkey's Paw*, is also based on the same idea.

A woman whose husband died as the result of chronic illness followed by an accident got hold of the idea that she had killed him, although she was quite blameless of any responsibility for his death. The false idea persisted in spite of all assurances from her family to the contrary. Eventually she had to be admitted to a mental hospital. This woman must have directed against her husband a hostile thought, which she had disowned and repressed into the unconscious because it conflicted with her more tender feelings for him. When her husband's death had made a reality of the hostile wish, she behaved as though she had killed him. Under the influence of the unconscious, which identified the wish with the deed, she held herself responsible for his death.

"On the occasions when the imaginary fulfilment of this wish," writes Dr Ernest Jones, "coincides with a real fulfilment brought about by some accident in the outer world, the person feels unconsciously just as responsible for the death, and just as guilty, as though he had actually committed murder."

(3) The third characteristic of the unconscious to which we wish to call attention is related to time. Besides being stored with the experiences of the past, the unconscious seems to be cognizant of the future.

A middle-aged woman related three "presentiments" which she had had during her life. The earliest of these dated back to the age of thirteen, when she was parting from her mother to return to boarding-school at the end of the holidays. Although her mother was in very good health at the time, the daughter had a presentiment that she would not see her again alive. The mother died before the end of the next term.

The second experience occurred when she was spoken to in the street by a young girl who was unknown to her. On parting from the girl, she had a strong urge to advise her not to talk to strangers. Although she afterwards tried to dismiss the thought, she could not get the girl out of her mind and felt uneasy about her without knowing why. Three weeks later she recognized the girl again by her photograph in the newspaper. She had been murdered.

After this the woman resolved that if she had such an experience again, she would not fail to warn the person concerned. Twelve months later a friend told her that he was trying to get a job for his grandson on the railway. She immediately advised him against it, because she felt convinced that the lad would have an accident and be killed. She even took the step of confiding in his grandfather about her presentiment of impending tragedy. The grandfather dismissed it as "imagination", and the boy applied for a job as porter and got it. A fortnight afterwards he fell between the platform and a moving train and was killed, knowing nothing about the fate that had been predicted for him.

It may seem far-fetched to suppose that the unconscious knew about these incidents in advance and attempted to warn the woman, but to put them down as due to coincidence is even more far-fetched. The writer prefers to think that in some way which we do not understand the unconscious has knowledge of future events, of which under certain circumstances we can become at least dimly aware.

Is the Will Free?

"If the unconscious mind knows what is going to happen in the future," the reader will ask, "what becomes of the notion of free will?" The writer's answer to this question is that he believes that the will itself, like other conscious mental processes, is determined by forces in the unconscious and is not free in any absolute sense.

For example, I say that to-morrow I will do such-and-such a thing, and then, when to-morrow comes, I do it. The traditional view is that I did it, as we say, "of my own free will". The determinist view, to which the writer subscribes, however, is that my conscious will to do it was itself determined by motives of which I remain unaware unless I take the trouble to analyse them.

Similarly, the traditional view would claim that I could have changed my decision and not have done the thing which I did, acting again "of my own free will". The determinist view, on the other hand, is that if I had changed my decision, that, too, would have been dictated by reasons of which I would remain equally unaware until I analysed them. Whichever course of action I take, therefore, is determined by unconscious forces which are erroneously attributed to the operation of "free" will.

The points that have been examined above do not exhaust the possibilities of the unconscious mind, or, if the reader wishes, the subjective and subconscious minds. At least they serve to give some indication that in its operation the unconscious is quite unlike the conscious mind. They encourage us to dig below the surface of mental life, and prevent us from being surprised if we find that things are not what they seem. "The deeper we probe in our study of mental processes," remarks Freud, "the more we become aware of the richness and complexity of their content." "The importance of the unconscious in actual life," adds Dr Jones, "is ... that *all* mental functioning originates in it; all our thoughts, interests, and conscious impulses leading to conduct have their source in the unconscious."

It must be emphasized, in conclusion, that these speculations are both tentative and incomplete. Consequently, they should be viewed with an open mind until the reader can confirm them from his own experience. He is recommended to study his own mental life, seeking from it illustrations of the points that have been made above. Only in this way will he come to acquire a really deep knowledge of human behaviour. He will be illuminating the latter by pursuing the quest of self-knowledge, which is the goal of psychology for the individual.

CHAPTER III

The Dream as Wish-fulfilment

OUR most direct knowledge of hidden mental processes has been obtained from the study of dreams, which have been described as "the royal road to the unconscious".

All early races laid stress on dreams and held them to be of great use. When Alexander the Great set out in search of conquest, men who were versed in dreams went with him. One night while he laid siege to the city of Tyre, he dreamed of a *satyr* who danced in triumph; his dream sages said that it foretold that he would take the city. Thereupon he gave the order to attack and Tyre fell as he had been told.

The chief work that has come down to us from the ancient world on the topic of dreams is that of Artemidorus, who is said to have lived at the time of the Emperor Hadrian (A.D. 76-138). His theory of dreams strikes a modern note. According to Artemidorus, the dream "happens in that instant when the affections are so vehement that they ascend up to the brain during our sleep, and meet with the more watchful spirits".

This quotation shows that its author recognized the presence of conflict in dreams. A further quotation from the same source anticipates the modern theory. "It happens also," continues Artemidorus, "that he that fasts all day, dreams at night that he is feeding; or if thirsty in the day-time, in the night-time he dreams of drinking."

Even before Artemidorus, Plato had said almost in the words of Freud: "In all of us, even in good men, there is a lawless wild-beast nature, which peers out in sleep."

A writer of the fourth century, Synesius of Cyrene, emphasized another value of dreams besides that of providing a "safety-valve" for our animal nature. He pointed out that we can gain from them useful knowledge about ourselves. "We do not sleep merely to live," he remarked, "but to learn to live well."

From his time till the close of the last century, however, a mass of false beliefs, which have not entirely been done away with even yet, gathered about the subject, which consequently sank into disrepute.

From this state it was rescued by the genius of Dr Sigmund Freud, the Viennese psychiatrist and founder of psycho-analysis, to whom we owe our modern knowledge of the subject. The statement that "the dream is the life of the mind during sleep" defines it in Freud's words, and repeats what Aristotle had said about its nature.

Sleep is a state in which interest is withdrawn from the outer world. We escape from it into a semblance of our pre-birth life. In sleep we often put ourselves in the shape that we knew before we came into the world—with our legs drawn up to the chin. Each morning we come into the world again as though we were being reborn.

Dreams show that the mind reacts in a certain way while we are asleep. Moreover it reacts in a way that may seem strange to us in waking life. We forget most dreams soon after waking; some stay with us, however, for a long time. A dream of childhood may be recalled as clearly in middle age as it was when it first occurred. They may recur or occur once only.

A WISH YOUR HEART MAKES

The psychological theory of dreams is that they are wish-fulfilments. A dream is the open or disguised fulfilment of a wish. For example, "I am often dreaming I am back at the bank where I used to work," stated a single girl of thirty. "I realize now I should have stayed at the bank," she added. "I often wish I were back."

The wish that appears in a dream may be either conscious or unconscious, *i.e.*, the dreamer may be aware of it or not. In the above example the dreamer was aware of her wish, which therefore merits being called conscious. At other times, however, the dreamer is not aware of it.

The idea that a dream represents the fulfilment of a wish finds an echo in the popular song, "A Dream is a Wish Your Heart Makes". Popular songs are, in fact, often a fertile source of simple illustrations of this theme. For example, in a song broadcast by Billy Cotton in the Band Show programme there occurred a reference to a sailor, who, having kissed his sweetheart good-bye on the jetty, subsequently dreamed that he was covered with confetti. We assume that his dream related, superficially at least, to his wish to marry the girl.

To convince ourselves of the truth of this proposition let us take a few more examples. Here are one or two examples of dreams which represent the fulfilment of conscious wishes.

A single 23-year-old clerk dreams: "I am at the home of a girl whom in real life I could not visit. I always had to meet her outside in the street. Now that I cannot see her again I dream ever so often that I am at her home."

The role of a dream as a wish-fulfilment is clearly apparent from this dream, which presents as fulfilled the dreamer's wish to visit the girl at her home.

When a person dreams that he is drinking long cooling draughts of water, he may wake up and find that he is thirsty. For instance, Mungo Park, the explorer, when nearly dying of thirst on a journey in Africa, dreamed continually of the well-watered hills and valleys of his home. We must suppose that the desire to quench his thirst translated itself during his sleep into this particular dream.

A young housewife, who desired a baby but had not succeeded after more than three years of marriage, dreamed: "I have a baby; the eyes are blue and he has lovely, golden curly hair. I nurse him and do everything that has to be done; then, when I wake up and find no baby, I could cry with disappointment. Each time I dream of this baby, the looks are always the same, but sometimes he is a small baby and sometimes a little boy of about four years."

In the early hours of a Friday morning, after a restless night during which he had not been feeling too well, the writer dreamed that it was Sunday. The wish not to go to work on account of being indisposed had evidently formed itself in the mind, and achieved expression as a dream which denied the reality of the need to go to work by saying: "It is Sunday; you can stay at home and rest."

The following dream was reported by a single 28-year-old clerk:

"I dreamed that my old girl-friend was at my office talking to one of the staff, who, I overheard, gave her two tickets for a dance to which she said she was looking forward. I opened the door for her and followed her out of the room, not knowing whether to hold my head in the air or smile. I smiled and she smiled back—the old smile that I knew when I meant something to her."

It is not difficult for us to cite this dream in support of the view that dreams are wish-fulfilments. The dreamer's ex-girl-friend used to smile at him when he meant something to her. In his dream she smiles at him again. Therefore in his dream he is seeking to convince himself that he still means something to her. The thought, "I wish we two were together again!" is implied by the two dance tickets.

REPRESSED WISHES

The dreams that we have cited so far have been found to reflect wishes of which the dreamer is more or less aware in his or her waking life. As the Hungarian proverb directly expresses it, "The hungry goose dreams of corn and the hungry pig of acorns." The great majority of dreams, however, have nothing whatever to do with conscious wishes, but reflect those which are deeply buried in the unconscious. Such wishes are said to be repressed.

A repressed wish is one that the dreamer refuses to acknowledge to himself. It is kept at an unconscious level, because it is held to be incompatible with conscious standards of thought and conduct. To admit it into consciousness would throw the individual into a mental conflict that he cannot tolerate.

Such unconscious wishes are frequently those that were entertained in childhood and that are no longer acceptable to the adult personality of the dreamer. He has repudiated them because they conflict with the standards to which his conscious mind subscribes. Even when these wishes receive indirect expression during sleep, they have to be heavily disguised before they can be permitted to emerge. This is why our dreams often seem to be of a nonsensical character.

We must, however, distinguish between the dream as it appears to the dreamer and the hidden wish to which it gives expression. The dream as it appears to the dreamer is known as the manifest content. This is the dream as it is remembered. The wishes and desires that provide the real meaning of the dream are known as the latent dream-thoughts.

The process by which the latent dream-thoughts are transformed into the manifest dream is called the dream-work. Although it is a form of thought, the dream-work differs from the ordinary everyday thought of the conscious mind in that it dispenses with logic and reason.

The work of interpretation consists in translating the manifest dream back into the latent dream-thoughts. "If the symbols commonly appearing in dreams are known," writes Freud, "and also the personality of the dreamer, the conditions under which he lives, and the impressions in his mind after which his dream occurred, we are often in a position to interpret it straight away; to translate it at sight, as it were."

In other cases we are compelled to ask the dreamer to tell us the thoughts and memories of which the dream reminds him. To use the proper term, we require him to give us his associations. By uncritically pursuing the associations arising from a dream one arrives at the latent dream-thoughts, which contain the meaning of the dream. In this way we encourage the dreamer to translate the dream for himself. Wherever possible it is desirable that this should occur, for if we try to force a meaning of our own upon the dream we may fall into grievous error.

"Psycho-analytic technique," Freud warns us, "endeavours as far as possible to let the persons being analysed give the answer to their own problems. The dreamer himself then should interpret his dream for us."

EXAMPLES

Here are some examples of dreams the interpretation of which is provided by the dreamer himself as a result of the associations which he gives to the dream.

A young man had the following dream: "I was standing by my girl-friend's mother's bed-side; she was very ill and I saw her die."

His associations were: "I was courting my girl, but we ceased going with each other because of a quarrel between her mother and myself. The row began because I was keeping late hours, because I was older than my girl, because I had a poorly-paid job, and, furthermore, because I didn't have an aim in life. When she said that I wasn't good enough for her daughter, this hit me hard. I brooded and gave much thought to her mother's words, finally coming to the conclusion that she was right."

The dreamer's correct interpretation of his own dream was: "I dreamed this because I believe she is the only person standing between ———— and myself, and if she were dead I would then have the girl whom I wanted."

A man of fifty dreamed: "I am at the helm of a sailing-boat, or on the bridge of a steamer." His association was: "I always wanted to go to sea, but a disability prevented it." In his dream he realized the wish that had been denied him in waking life. The dream attempted to compensate him for his frustrated ambition.

A 26-year-old single girl dreamed: "I was having a quarrel with my family. I aimed a blow at my mother and brother. My brother fell and that was the end of it." The associations containing the meaning of her dream were: "I feel hostile to my family. My brother is at times unbearable."

A woman who was devoted to her mother dreamed that the latter had disappeared and that she was not allowed to look for her. The dreamer, who had married somewhat above her social rank, was ashamed of the district in which her mother lived, and was afraid that in her higher social circle she might meet someone who knew that district. The dream of her mother disappearing and herself making no effort to find her attempted to gratify her wish to overcome her fear by having her mother move elsewhere. "I am sure that if my mother would move," she said, "all my fears would vanish."

LEAVE IT TO FATHER

A 37-year-old man reported the following dream: "I was operating my radio station and actually in contact with a well-known person—everything being very correct and real."

"I had better explain here," he added, "that I hold an amateur transmitting licence, and when possible can spend very enjoyable hours building and operating the station, but have not had it working for some time owing to domestic commitments."

The interpretation, in his own words, was: "This is interpreted as just a genuine wish to get 'on the air', as we call it, again as soon as possible. I have actually rather purposely put this in the background a bit, and have not visited the local club lately, in order to try and get other things done for the family, including the construction of a television receiver."

This interpretation leaves obscure the identity of the well-known person with whom the dreamer is in contact. The dreamer's identification with his father was revealed in another dream and the associations which he reported. The dream was: "I had returned to my old and original job." He added: "My father is in the same line."

A tendency to rely on his father for the solution of his problems seems to be reflected in a further dream of his: "Father and I had entered premises unlawfully at night. We were disturbed by the unexpected arrival of night-workers. I was surprised to find, however, that father had miraculously completed the job."

The dreamer complained that he had a life-long total lack of confidence. After moving away from his home town to take another post, he "allowed the job to get him down." This led to his selling the house he had bought and returning home again.

The identity of the well-known person who figures in his first dream may, therefore, be the father upon whom he depends in the absence of confidence in his own abilities.

CHAPTER IV

Dreams of Birth

A THEME that appears frequently in dreams is the wish to return to the blissful state of life before we were born. It is easy to see in such dreams the expression of escapism. By yearning to return to the comfort and security of our mother's body, the child within us seeks to escape from the burdens and responsibilities of adult life.

A single 52-year-old housekeeper has a dream that takes four forms. In the first, she says, "I am walking along a passage in daylight; the passage narrows until I cannot get through." The second one is: "I am going upstairs and the ceiling is so near the stairs that I cannot get past." These two are the least terrifying forms of the dream. Nevertheless she wakes in terror.

A more terrifying form, from which she wakes in a panic and has to keep the light on, is as follows: "I am in a room and the only way out is a narrow passage I cannot get my head through." At its worst she dreams: "I am in the dark lying on my back with my head wedged in something; my jaw is pushed out and my neck bent back." After this dream she wakes in terror, feels ill all day, and is afraid to go to sleep the next night. "I don't forget these dreams," she adds.

Her further associations are: "This is a nightmare that I have had all my life, although it has troubled me much more the last year or so, and is getting to be an obsession during the day. I have always been very nervous and sensitive. Just recently I have been trying to trace the cause of the dream, as it has worried me so much. I thought perhaps it was caused by reading at the age of eight a tale of being buried alive, but I had the dream or rather the *memory* before that. Then one day I thought, 'That is just what I should remember of being born'; since then the terror has left me a little, and I have been able to put the dream into words—a thing I was quite unable to do before, although I have wanted to write about it for a long time. Is it at all possible for anyone to have a memory of birth?"

It is unusual for a person to have so much insight into the meaning of his own dream. The dreams may correspond to the actual experience of being born, or they may be based on the memory of an early fantasy about returning to the womb. The former likelihood might be confirmed if the dreamer's actual birth was a difficult one. Invited to get confirmation of this point from her mother, the dreamer subsequently informed me: "I most certainly had a difficult birth and nearly died at the time."

When making this statement she added: "I shall not be so worried the next time I have the dream, and have to a large extent lost the day-time obsession with the subject." Some time afterwards she reported: "I am pleased to say that I no longer have the nightmare of being in a small space since I gained insight into its meaning."

THE DARK TUNNEL

Sometimes the details of this dream vary, but in essence the dream is the same. For example, a married 50-year-old man dreamed of crawling through a narrow confined space. He was advised that such dreams are not at all uncommon, and that they reflect a very early memory of the dreamer's life—the experience of being born.

The dreamer later wrote: "I don't know how you arrived at the explanation of my dream of escaping through a small space in the pit. The fact is that my birth was difficult, and still I have the marks of the doctor's instruments on my forehead."

"I used to dream that I was crawling through a dark tunnel or up inside a drain pipe," stated a 35-year-old housewife. She herself offered the correct interpretation of her dream by asking: "Was this being born?"

A 31-year-old housewife adds the detail of water: "I had the dream of trying to get out of a dark tunnel full of water. I was crawling through it, and as I reached the end of it I woke up in a panic." "The symbolic significance of water," writes Dr Ernest Jones, "is mainly derived from its unconscious equivalency with uterine fluid ... it is probably the commonest symbol ... employed in birth fantasies."

A 42-year-old cashier reports a dream in which this element predominates: "I often used to dream of being cut off by floods or tides and stranded, and once in particular I saw a great wall of sea coming towards me. The other night in bed I suddenly had an awful sensation of being surrounded by floods of water."

"My most frequent dreams," adds another person, "concern squeezing through very small confined spaces, *e.g.*, coal-mines, etc." She volunteers the further information that she has no fear of small spaces when awake, but admits that she is rather tall and that at school she was very conscious of her height.

The wish to be small again—so small, in fact, as to be able to return to our life before birth—also receives temporary gratification in the everyday act of retiring to bed and falling asleep. Some people curl themselves up in bed into as small a space as possible. The position which they adopt resembles that of the child in the mother's body.

One question that raises itself at this point is: Why should we need to dream about returning to our life before birth when sleep itself attempts to gratify this wish? It may be because when we lie curled up in bed we do not exactly reproduce the conditions of pre-birth existence. Consequently, the wish to return to that state is not fully satisfied. For example, we ordinarily wear clothes during sleep, whereas the child comes into the world in his "birthday suit".

Writing in the Sunday press, the author of an article on "How I Cured Nightmares" describes how he got rid of nightmares with the same content as those described in this chapter. He did this by the simple expedient of sleeping unclothed. The reason why this strategy succeeded is, perhaps, that by lying unclothed in bed he gratified in a more realistic manner the fantasy of returning to the womb. Hence he ceased to experience the need to gratify this fantasy by means of his nightmares.

In dreams of birth we may observe how the unconscious mind introduces details of the child's anatomy of which the dreamer in his conscious waking life may not even be aware. Here is a dream in which this is illustrated:

"An enormous hole had been bored in my head, and I could see myself diminutive in stature lying on my stomach on my dream-head. I was clutching the edge of this crater and staring over a black depthless precipice. All the time a terrific whirring noise prevailed, as if a drill were being used."

It is of interest to note that at birth the child has a hole in the crown of the head. This is known as the fontanelle and it gradually closes up as the bones of the skull grow and knit together. To dream of oneself as diminutive in stature is, of course, to dream of oneself as a child. The dream re-enacts the birth of the dreamer, the crater and deep precipice symbolizing the entrance to the external world. The latter, from the child's point of view, is "a great big blooming, buzzing confusion", as the psychologist William James has described it.

SCARED OF LIFE

A young married man had been discharged from H.M. Forces on account of nervous debility. He complained of a fear of the future and suffered from depression and loss of self-control.

One of his dreams was: "I feel as if I am either enclosed in a box or paralysed all over, unable to move a muscle. Finding myself suffocating, I try to get my body moving to reach the fresh air. This I eventually do after a great struggle."

The associations which he reported were: "The box is life and I am suffocating in trying to escape from it. I get very scared of life if I let my mind dwell on it. When I get depressed and fed up with life, I want to run away from it all—a feeling that if I get out into the country I could leave everything behind. Maybe the solution of the dream lies in the fact that, whilst I am at times so terrified of life, I know I have to stick it."

The dreamer also recalled a visit to the cemetery where his father was lying. He referred to "that inevitable day when I also shall be in a similar position." "I cannot believe that he is gone," he added.

The son, who dreams of lying in a box, recalls that his father is doing the same. Therefore his dream means that he identifies himself with his father. In other words, since his father is dead, the dream expresses the thought, "I wish that I too were dead." As he admits that he is afraid of life, this seems a reasonable conclusion to draw.

To be dead also implies the idea of not having been born—to be still unborn, like the child in the womb. We shall have occasion to note in a later chapter the significance of any object enclosing a space, such as a box. The dream-mind may make use of such an object as a symbol of the mother's womb—the source of the life of which the dreamer is afraid. In *The Interpretation of Dreams* Freud mentions that this meaning is given in popular speech to the German word for "box".

Readers of Edgar Allan Poe's weird and macabre stories will recall that his tale of *The Pit and the Pendulum* portrays the anxiety associated with the threat of having one's rest in a closed space disturbed by an intrusion or by the closing in of the walls of the space.

The content of this story is derived from the same unconscious source as the dreams in which this theme also appears. It comes from childhood fantasies about the pre-natal state. The pit in the story or the confined space in the dreams represents the mother's body. The closing in of the pit walls stands for the muscular contractions of the walls of the womb. These lead to the process of birth, which expels the child from his pre-natal Eden.

Judging from the anxiety which is associated with the above dream, we might assume that the dreamer is afraid of suffocating or of being unable to move. The dream, however, attempts to satisfy the fantasy of hiding in a place of safety and comfort. As the dreamer tells us, he is there because he is afraid of life. The anxiety arises from the threat of expulsion. As a married 30-year-old press operator described it: "I dream of being in a room which gets smaller until I can't breathe, and then I wake up." The walls of the womb (room) contract to expel the infant, who does not commence to breathe until after he is born.

The pre-birth life of comfort and security in the mother's womb is also the ultimate source of our ideas of the Garden of

Eden and of a life of everlasting bliss after death. We surmise that the individual experiences the first nine months of his existence as a period of endless duration, upon which are based our views about eternity. This need not surprise us when we realize that biologically the individual retraces in the first nine months the whole course of the evolution of life. The foetus passes through in miniature all the stages of development which have culminated in the appearance of man on this planet.

In a footnote to page 400 of the work quoted above we read that these "phantasies and unconscious thoughts about life in the womb ... contain an explanation of the remarkable dread that many people have of being buried alive; and they also afford the deepest unconscious basis for the belief in survival after death, which merely represents a projection into the future of this uncanny life before birth."

CHAPTER V

Dreams of Death

THE subject-matter of dreams is limited to a handful of themes, namely, the great mysteries of life such as procreation, birth and death. Let us, therefore, turn from the dreams that deal with birth to the equally common ones that concern themselves with death.

The person who meets his death in our dreams is apt to be someone to whom our attitude in waking life appears to be just the reverse of hostility. That person may be someone of whom we are very fond, such as a child, a husband or wife, or perhaps a close relative like mother or father. We may be tempted to suppose that the wish-fulfilment theory of dreams breaks down at this point. How, we may ask ourselves, could we wish for the death of someone who is dear to us?

For example, a single 26-year-old locomotive fireman dreamed that his father was dead.

We must be careful to distinguish the affection which he no doubt *consciously* felt for his father from the *unconscious* hostility which is gratified by imagining his death. The fact that the conscious affection is tempered with the unconscious hostility need not surprise us, when we realize that this occurs in almost all cases of intense devotion to a particular person.

Its occurrence is proved by the fact that when a person who is in love is rejected by his loved one, his intense devotion may suddenly turn into the most bitter hatred. This was, of course, there all the time, but was kept carefully repressed, so that the individual remained unaware of it.

In the case of a son's attitude towards his father, this "ambivalence" (love combined with hatred) has its origin in the former's childhood. Then the son, besides looking up to his father with awe and respect, also sees in him a rival for the attention of his mother.

LOVE AND HATRED

Here are some further illustrations of ambivalence. The first is a report from a single 22-year-old man: "*I loved a girl very deeply, but my hopes of having her for my wife were dashed. Now I snub her* at every opportunity I get."

A woman of forty-six said that she had "*ached and longed*" for her mother to come over from Canada to visit her; yet when her mother arrived the woman admitted that she "*failed to show her much affection.*" "I clearly remember going with her to Liverpool when she was sailing," she stated, "and *parting from her in the most offhand manner;* yet *my whole being longed to hold her tight.*"

Referring to her relationship with her brother, a 31-year-old factory worker declared: "We were *very affectionate* to each other, but *often quarrelled violently.*" Reviewing certain incidents in his past life, a young man admitted: "When I had been *sobbing my heart out,* I had been *smiling* too."

A single 23-year-old girl said that she *got her temper up only with people who meant the most to her.* "I say vile and horrible things that I don't mean," she acknowledged. "I know I don't mean them even when I'm saying them, but I do it to hurt people. The person I have hurt most of all is my mother, and yet she is everything in the world to me. When strangers or associates annoy me I just ignore them."

A young man described his behaviour as follows: "I am working in a kitchen where I got very friendly with one of the staff—a girl. *I am very fond of her,* and when she is not around I speak well of her. But when she comes into the kitchen, or when I see or meet her anywhere on the premises, *I ignore her completely.* I won't speak to her, won't bid her good morning, *and insult her in front of everyone.* This lasts about a fortnight, then I relax and apologize, saying it won't happen again. But within a couple of weeks I am off again."

In all these examples we see the existence side by side of conflicting attitudes towards the same person. This is what we mean when we speak of "ambivalence". Anyone who hitherto has doubted the possibility of his both loving and hating the same person need no longer remain unconvinced after studying them.

Ambivalence is especially characteristic of childhood as well as of the dreams and waking experiences of adults. It is a feature of the child's attitude towards his mother, who is for him the source of both satisfaction and frustration. The mother satisfies the child by feeding, clothing, nursing and protecting him, but she also frustrates him by weaning, toilet-training, chiding and spanking him.

"In Self-Defence"

A 61-year-old woman reports: "When I was five, on the first night we were in —————, where my parents and I went to live, I dreamed that my father was run over and killed. His body was brought home on a square-based trolley (a miniature of the kind used by electricians to test and repair electric road standards), all neatly folded up like clothes in which there was no body!"

We observe that this dream attempts to disguise the death-wish by denying the presence of the body. It says, as it were: "There really is no dead body—it's just a pile of clothes!"

A housewife reported the following dream: "I dreamed that I killed a man who was trying to steal a key. I battered him with a shovel; there was blood all over it. I did not mean to kill him, but did it in self-defence. Then I saw a waxwork-like figure of a woman strutting stiff-legged across the room."

The dreamer reported that she worried because her husband preferred drinking with other men to taking her out. Although she did not doubt his love, she felt that he did not show it as she would like him to do. Her husband had obtained a fairly well-to-do material position, although, since he kept her short of money, this was not of much advantage to her.

The man who is killed in the dream is evidently her husband, who she believes holds the key to her happiness. She has reason to harbour aggressive wishes against him, since she has complained that he neglects her. The expression of her aggressiveness against her husband is condoned by her killing him in self-defence.

The dream also contains the punishment for the death-wish, and illustrates the primitive unconscious justice and retribution of "an eye for an eye and a tooth for a tooth". Her husband's death must be paid for by her own death. She herself is depicted in the dream as a "stiff" with the wax-like features of the dead. No doubt, too, we have here an expression of the thought of "stiffening" with horror at the thought of thus disposing of her husband.

This dream apparently provided a much-needed safety-valve for the dreamer's hostility against her husband. The recognition of its meaning enabled her to accept her hostility and even to smile at it. Her comments were: "Well, it was rather a shock. But I *have* harboured aggressive thoughts. I realize these are wrong now and will chase them out whenever they come. After the first shock I feel tickled to think I killed him in my dream. I will try and be better."

Later she reported: "I have not had one aggressive thought against my husband since you told me I was killing him in my dream."

CRIME AND PUNISHMENT

A professional boxer had dreams of "committing a murder". "Such things are very terrible to me when I wake," he stated. "Sometimes I even dread to sleep for fear that I might do these things, and so I have a sleepless night at times."

It is obvious that this man had aggressive and sadistic wishes that found an outlet in these dreams. The existence of such wishes also throws light on his choice of boxing as a career. This activity provided an outlet in waking life for the wishes that appear in his dreams. It enabled him to inflict pain and indulge in brutality in a socially acceptable way.

Boxing also permitted him to have pain and brutality inflicted upon himself. That self-contrived punishment sought to atone for the sense of guilt aroused by the existence of the wishes expressed in the dreams. This sense of guilt was also satisfied by another set of dreams that he had. In these he "dreamed of being in prison". The dreams of being in prison were psychologically related to the dreams of committing murder. The one represented the "punishment" for the "crime" of the other. The dreams of murder seek to gratify the wild untamed impulses of the unconscious, while the dreams of prison express the wish of the conscious mind to control and punish such impulses.

Instead of appearing in separate dreams, the two elements may be combined in the same dream, which then represents both the "crime" and the "punishment" for it. For example, "I have mostly unpleasant dreams in which I find myself in serious trouble," states a single 26-year-old machine operator, "such as being wanted by the police for killing someone or for doing some serious damage, although in real life I've never been in trouble with the police."

The danger of being caught by the police in this dream performs the same psychological function as the imprisonment in the above dreams.

"Most people at some time in their lives," says a young man, "most especially in a moment of anger, have said, 'I could *kill* that person!' Less than one in a thousand ever carries out such a threat, but the 'bad' thought has been uttered."

We should remember that to the infantile self which speaks in dreams "kill" simply means "get out of the way". To the young child "kill" conveys no more than the idea of getting rid of something or someone undesirable. Each of us carries round with him an infantile part that achieves expression in dreams of death in spite of the disapproval of the adult part of himself.

CHAPTER VI

Terror in the Night

FROM two of the examples quoted in the last chapter we have seen how a dream may depict not only a "crime" but also the "punishment" for it. In other words, it forms a compromise which satisfies the claims of both the unconscious and the conscience or moral self. Sometimes, however, the wish on the part of the unconscious may seem to be suppressed altogether, so that only the wish on the part of the conscience emerges from the dream. This means that the dream presents the "punishment" without the crime.

This may throw light on dreams which are unpleasant and anxiety-provoking, and which therefore seem to contradict the definition of a dream proposed in chapter III.

For example, a single 41-year-old factory worker dreamed almost the same dream several times between 1946 and 1951. It was that he had gone back to Poland—and back to the forced labour camp in Russia which he left in reality in 1942. "I meet there," he added, "the people whom I left—and they say to me how stupid I am coming back again."

Dreams of this type that are attended by anxiety and have an unpleasant content raise a general problem in dream psychology. We said at the outset that a dream is a fulfilment of a wish. Why then, we may ask ourselves, should anyone wish to undergo unpleasant experiences in his dreams?

Surely, if dreams are wish-fulfilments we are entitled to assume that their content should be invariably pleasant. What happens to our theory of dreams if we admit the existence of unpleasant dreams that provoke anxiety?

This question, as I hope to show you, can be answered in more than one way, but first of all let me give you a few more examples.

ON THE FERRY-BOAT

A 59-year-old housewife reported the "same dream in different dress three times—being in a ship—going over dry land—then back again into deep waters." That this dream repeats an unpleasant experience may be seen from the dreamer's associations, which were: "I *know* the origin. Once, as a child, I went on a Sunday-school treat to ————; on our return the ferry-boat was caught on a sandbank for over an hour (I experienced childhood fear)—then as the tide rose we lifted off the sandbank. My mother met me (also full of fears) and this impression (to me) must have been deeper than I knew at the time."

Another dreamer records: "I am struggling with window frames which are loose and sometimes come right out of place. I am in such a great fear that I cannot get them back in place and that they will fall into the street below."

The writer is indebted to an Australian source for the following case.

A young married woman had been disturbed by a very vivid nightmare almost from the time of her marriage. The dream always followed the same pattern: she, or some other person, was always chasing her husband with an axe, knife, or other dangerous weapon.

The nightmare caused sleeplessness, which in turn produced a headache; this again caused sleeplessness, and so a vicious circle was set up.

Even a limited knowledge of dream-analysis will suggest some unconscious resentment on the dreamer's part towards her husband. This fact was confirmed under hypnosis. Hypnotic suggestion was combined with an explanation. This treatment removed all the symptoms, which did not afterwards return.

A dream with an unpleasant content may repeat some unpleasant experience which the dreamer has suffered in the past and in which he has played a purely passive role. That is to say, it is something that he has had happen to him. By repeating the experience in his dreams, he assumes command of the situation and gratifies the desire to change his role from passive to active. It then becomes something that he causes to happen.

Small Fry

"I remember," stated a man, "that we once had at school a boy who was eventually expelled. He was a rough sort of beggar, fond of bullying small boys. One day I saw him twisting a small boy's arm, causing him great pain, and I blurted out: 'Pack that up, you bully!' He let go the little boy, turned and struck me across the face. *I stood there rigid and did nothing about it.*"

This memory was recalled in connection with the following dream: "A big fish was trying to bite a little fish. I hit the big fish with a lump of wood to try to stop it."

The retaliation depicted in the dream contrasts with the inaction of the real event, and illustrates the wish-fulfilment that converts the dreamer's role from passive to active.

One also notes in connection with the dream that youngsters are called "small fry", while older and more important individuals are called "big fry". This term, which originally refers to young fish, especially those fresh from the spawn, throws light on the choice of fish to represent the schoolboy participants.

We may also call attention to the figurative use of the word "fish" in descriptions of human beings, *e.g.*, a poor fish, an odd fish, a fish out of water.

The same person also reported another incident from childhood in relating a similar dream. This, too, repeated an unpleasant experience and modified the dreamer's role. "When I was quite small," he recounts, "I remember an even smaller and insignificant child unexpectedly throwing me on my back. I found that he had me in such a grip that I was powerless to move."

This experience, which the narrator described as "devastating", was recalled as an association to the following dream: "Some sort of object settled on my chest, but I shifted it after a great struggle."

From Passive To Active

This "urge to repeat" is a general tendency that plays an important part in human nature. We repeat actively what we have experienced passively not only in dreams but also in waking life.

For example, a woman stated that her married life was marred by serious quarrels. "Always I wanted to get away," she added, "and sometimes did go away and devised other means of hurting my husband." A study of her background showed that she had had a father who ill-treated her as a child. She described her childhood as "very unhappy". She had married her husband in order to provide herself with someone upon whom she could revenge herself for the suffering which she had experienced at the hands of her father.

In her marriage she repeated the situation of her childhood but changed her own role from passive to active. She actively inflicted on her husband the suffering which she had passively experienced from her father.

When a person is made to do something whether he likes it or not, that person suffers a blow to his self-esteem. The purpose of the urge to repeat actively what we have experienced passively is to eradicate this blow. An individual restores his self-esteem by saying to himself, as it were: "I am doing this because I say so, and not because someone else says so." We all like to feel that we are free to act as we wish within the limits of the law and the dictates of common sense.

A 47-year-old housewife described her husband as "a lovable child". "I have always looked upon him as a son," she added, "who is in need of constant guidance. I love him because of his dependence. I pushed him in and out of jobs. I tell him exactly what to do and when to do it."

This woman's mother was an extremely neurotic person who, when her daughter was born, lavished an abnormal adoration on her to compensate herself for the frustration of her emotions by her own unhappy marriage. "She possessed me," the daughter stated. "She could not bear me out of her sight." In her own marriage the daughter unconsciously turned the tables by treating her husband as she had been treated by her mother.

A man was ridiculed as a child by his father. He said: "I seem to hold myself open as a target for ridicule from my workmates." What he meant was that he *actively* provoked his workmates to ridicule him in order to counteract the ridicule that he had suffered *passively* from his father without being able to do anything about it.

CHAPTER VII

The Night-watchman

UNPLEASANT dreams attended by anxiety generally awake us, as we have seen from the examples given at the beginning of chapter IV. We usually break off our sleep before the repressed wish behind the dream reaches complete fulfilment. As one dreamer put it, "It's such a relief to know that I can wake up from it." By "it" he referred to a dream "of a terrible danger or a major catastrophe in my life."

Psycho-analysis has compared the dream to a night-watchman whose purpose it is to protect sleep from interruption. This is the guardianship theory. Now night-watchmen have to wake sleepers when they are not strong enough to ward off the danger alone. Nevertheless, we do sometimes succeed in continuing to sleep even when our dreams begin to cause us distress.

We say to ourselves, as did a single 31-year-old electrician, "While dreaming, if anything very unpleasant happens to me, I frequently tell myself—'You are only dreaming', and feel relieved without waking. In other words, I dream that I tell myself, 'You are only dreaming'. This has happened quite a few times."

"If the dream is really horrible," stated a married 44-year-old rent collector, "I think, even in the dream, 'Ah, well, it's only a dream—I shall wake up soon'."

A married woman of thirty-one attempted to deal with her anxiety in both ways. Sometimes she woke up, but often she dreamed that she was only dreaming. "I have plenty of night-mares," she said. "For instance, I dream that my children are either murdered, drowned, or lying under a bus. *Sometimes I wake up with a thumping head and wet with perspiration. Often, however, I know that I am dreaming and can tell myself that it is only a dream and that I shall wake up in a minute.*"

"OUT IN THE COLD, COLD SNOW"

Besides dealing with causes of anxiety in the mind itself, the night-watchman also attempts to ward off outside stimuli. Anything that threatens to wake up the sleeper and thus deprive him of the rest that sleep confers is made an occasion for a dream. In this way the watchman attempts to ensure that the dreamer shall go on sleeping.

This is illustrated by the following example:

"My husband dreamed that it was snowing. He woke up very cold."

The fact that the husband was cold may have provoked the dream. By bringing about a dream the dream-mind tries to prevent the cold from waking the husband, for as long as he goes on dreaming he cannot awaken. The intensity of the cold was probably such that the dream-mind was not successful in making him go on sleeping. The dreamer was awakened by the cold in spite of its being converted into a dream of snow. This does not altogether explain the dream, of course, but merely throws light on its sources of origin.

A story by Enid Blyton opens with a ball thrown by a little boy falling on a Mr Shouter, who is asleep in a deck-chair. "The ball fell bang on Mr Shouter's head," we read, "and in his dreams he thought a bomb had fallen on him."

The insertion of this dream, which is in no way essential to the story, is a detail of considerable interest. Whether the authoress is familiar with the guardianship theory of dreams or not, it reveals a good deal of psychological insight on her part.

The impact of the ball on the man's head would tend to wake him up. The dream-mind converts it into a dream of a bomb explosion, which attempted to preserve the dreamer's sleep. The simulus was such, however, that the dream-mind did not succeed in this aim, with the result that Mr Shouter awoke.

The attempt to preserve sleep in the face of the disturbing stimulus explains why the dream occurred. The particular form that the dream took, however, was related to the dreamer's psychology. We are told that Mr Shouter had a very grievous temper. The aggressive impulses that he harboured took the form of threats to spank the little boy, put him through the mangle, iron him flat, peg him on the line and beat him like a carpet. The impact of the ball was converted into a dream of a bomb explosion because the dreamer himself was constantly on the verge of exploding with rage. Besides serving the purpose of attempting to safeguard sleep, the dream in the particular form that it took sought to find an outlet for the dreamer's aggressive hostility.

HEAD NOISES

How sleep is preserved against the threat of interruption by head noises is illustrated by the dream of a single 37-year-old housekeeper. She dreamed: "I was back in my home town, when I met my brother standing by the sea-wall and talking to a young lady whom he introduced to me. As he and I walked away from her he told me in a roundabout fashion that he was not happy, and all the time we were talking the sea was roaring in mountainous waves."

The dreamer stated that this dream reminded her of her childhood. "I frequently used to dream," she added, "that I was walking over the sea, or I used to be walking up in the air above people's heads. I have got into financial difficulties. I am troubled with head noises. My brothers and sisters ignore me because I behave so stupidly."

The head noises that trouble her during the day also threaten to disturb her sleep. In order to prevent her waking up and thus losing valuable rest, the dream-mind converts them into a dream of roaring seas, which also express the idea that she is "all at sea" on account of her "stupid" behaviour.

The dream also gratifies the girl's wish to be taken notice of by her brother and to have him prefer her company even to that of his young lady. This is understandable in view of the fact that the dreamer's brother had ignored her in real life. By making her home town its setting and by introducing the sea, about which she used to dream frequently as a child, the dream also says, "You are a child again." This is a further wish-fulfilment, for if she were a child again she would be freed from the difficulties of adult life that have tended to be too much for her.

There is also an element of revenge in the dream, which says, in effect, "I wish my brother were unhappy too; then he would know how I feel." The dream has no other means of depicting this wish than by actually having the dreamer's brother confess his unhappiness. In this way, too, the wish is disguised by making it appear that the dreamer knew nothing about it until her brother told her. In reality, however, she knew about it all the time, for she understood clearly in spite of her brother's round-about explanation.

Just as sleep is essential to health, so it may be said that dreams are essential to sleep. Mind and body are very much dependent upon each other, and if for some reason the body fails to receive its proper ration of sleep, the mind is quick to enter a protest. When the memories of the past threaten to break into conscious-ness and interrupt our sleep, they are dressed up in the symbolic language of the unconscious and are manifested in the guise of dreams.

Dreams enable us to remain asleep when the activity of the mind tends to wake us up. Sometimes, however, a particularly disturbing thought succeeds in breaking through. Such an event is the origin of a "bad" dream and the "night terrors" of our childhood days. The hints that will be given in the next chapter on overcoming insomnia will be found useful in dealing with these additional disturbances of rest. As physical and mental hygiene is practised, so will sleep intensify in value.

CHAPTER VIII

Safeguarding our Sleep

IT is one of the paradoxes of life that in order to enjoy it fully we should spend at least one third of it in sleep. For at least eight hours' sleep a day is a necessity for the human body.

This statement assumes that you are between fifteen and fifty years of age. Those who are younger than fifteen may expect to sleep more, while those who are older than fifty may expect to sleep less. The average daily period spent in sleep decreases from about twenty-two hours at birth to about nine hours at the age of fourteen. Beyond the age of fifty the average daily period drops sharply to about six hours at the age of sixty, and over the age of sixty-five it may be only as little as three or four hours.

Of course, both these ages and these amounts are approximate. Differences may be observed from one person to another. The changes in an individual's sleeping habits are normally gradual rather than sudden.

Whatever our age, though, sleep is of importance especially if our waking hours impose a heavy burden of strain both mental and physical on our resources, overtaxing us with their demands from day to day.

Important as they may be, however, it would be a mistake to exaggerate the effects of the loss of sleep on efficiency. They are not as serious as we have perhaps been led to believe in some quarters. Laboratory studies show that, when work after normal sleep is compared with work after wakefulness, the difference is relatively small.

Nevertheless, sleep is as essential to the human body as is food; in fact, it is more essential, for the human machine can keep working for a longer time without food than it can without sleep. Experiments conducted on dogs by the German physiologist Kleitmann have shown that during a period of enforced abstinence from sleep the percentage of red corpuscles in the dogs' blood diminished by one quarter, and that although dogs can live for as long as three weeks without food, young puppies die in a week without sleep.

WHAT IS SLEEP?

Sleep has been the subject of much investigation and research by psychologists, who have endeavoured to arrive at a statement of its purpose and nature. An early pronouncement crystallized in the adage, "Six hours for a man, seven for a woman, and eight for a fool", is, as shown above, not to be taken too seriously. Among modern investigators Pavlov has clearly demonstrated that in sleep the brain is engaged in ceaseless activity, even when the sleeper may apparently be quite unconscious. But sleep has never been summed up with greater eloquence or exactitude than in the many tributes paid to it in poetry and song, of which the following from the pen of the author of *Night Thoughts* is typical:

"Tired Nature's sweet restorer, balmy sleep."

There in a nutshell is what sleep really is.

It is interesting to observe that sleep is a part of the rhythm of the universe, and that it demonstrates the universal law of compensation, which states that for every action there is a reaction. The activity of the day is followed by the repose of sleep at night. The new birth and growth of spring follow the quiescent period of winter. The chrysalis of the short dark days is the butterfly of the long sunny days.

Sleep also serves the purpose of helping to banish the cares and anxieties of the day just passed and of the days before that. This is what E. M. H. Gates seems to be thinking of in the verse which decorates many a bedroom wall:

"Sleep sweet within this quiet room,
O thou! whoe'er thou art;
And let no mournful Yesterday
Disturb thy peaceful heart."

It is not always possible for everyone to obtain the full ration of eight hours' sleep each day—or whatever amount is normal for our age. It is, therefore, all the more important to make the utmost use of the sleep that we do get. How are we to do this?

37

AIDS TO SLEEP

The old-fashioned "remedy" for sleeplessness was the administering of drugs and "sleeping-draughts". This is very much like attempting to cure constipation by means of cathartics. Both methods are ineffective and habit-forming. What is more important is to adjust the mode of life.

An invaluable aid in overcoming insomnia is to tone up the physical health to the highest possible pitch by observing the ordinary laws of health and diet. It is also advisable to get as much fresh air as possible, and when you are out in the open air to breathe in deeply. The exercise of deep breathing is one of the most health-giving both mentally and physically.

The inability to sleep properly is one of the prices which man has had to pay for the benefits of civilization. His primitive ancestors, whose lives were spent in fleeing from danger or in hunting for food, were so tired out by the physical pursuits of the day, that it never occurred to them that they might not be able to sleep at the end of it.

To-day the majority of us spend our lives in greater mental activity than muscular exercise. Instead of going out to hunt for our food we worry about what the butcher will send us. Instead of fleeing for safety from our enemies we keep the wolf from the door by bending over desks and entering figures in a ledger. Consequently, we are not nearly so physically tired at the end of the day as we are mentally active. The body quite naturally does not feel the need of sleep, and when we go to bed, instead of relaxing, we very unwisely allow the over-active mind free rein to churn over the events of the day just passed to the detriment of sleep and rest.

Unless this tendency is checked it can easily become a habit, so that we wake up in the morning more tired than when we went to bed, what sleep we have had having failed in its primary purpose to recreate us in order to face the coming day. At least one nationally-known firm has "cashed in" on this weakness in human nature in its advertisements for a certain brand of "night-cap".

It has truly been said that when worry comes in at the window sleep flies out at the door. Those sufferers from insomnia who have not learned to exercise thought-control in overcoming worry should do so without delay. This technique of mental hygiene consists of meeting every thought of worry and anxiety with a constructive thought of success and well-being, until a strong positive thought habit is built up that will replace the old negative habit. It is the surest remedy for worry and consequently a very effective cure for insomnia. Those who are of a religious turn of mind will drive out worry with inspiring thoughts such as that in sleep they are re-created in the pulsating bosom of the Creative Intelligence, and will share in the hope expressed by the hymnwriter that his sleep will make him more vigorous to serve his God when awake.

A hot drink of milk in bed the last thing at night is one of the most effective soporifics. Countless numbers of people have been sent to sleep by this simple little remedy for insomnia. Even if the milk does not send you to sleep, it will still do you good, for milk contains valuable vitamins and is rich in mineral salts.

The last half-hour before retiring should be spent in a soothing and relaxing atmosphere. All troubles of the day should be put out of the mind. Compose yourself in a comfortable chair to read a book or listen to the radio programme. This last-minute rest will take your mind right away from the petty little cares and troubles which harass all of us in our daily lives. Always have a good wash, or even a bath if convenient before retiring; it has the effect of soothing jaded nerves. Always sleep with a window open, except in foggy weather. It not only helps to induce sleep, but is excellent for the general health.

SHOULD WE READ IN BED?

Reading for a short time in bed can be very helpful, providing that suitable reading material of a restful nature is chosen. A book that was brought to my notice the other day seems to have been designed for this purpose, since it contains a selection of extracts of prose and verse of an inspirational and devotional character. But any book of a similar type will do, and here the selection may safely be left with the individual. Some will choose the Bible, while with others Shakespeare will find favour. Shakespeare must have suffered from insomnia, for no one has praised sleep, "balm of hurt minds", so much as he.

The habit of reading in bed is supposed to be damaging to the eyes, but, provided the light is good, there is no reason why it should be any more damaging than reading in a sitting posture. The danger is not that it will injure the eyes, but that one who reads a detective thriller or a "blood" in bed will be tempted to read on into the small hours and thus rob himself of sleep. The reading of books of an exciting or engrossing nature is, therefore, to be discouraged.

Those who have sufficient faith may care to avail themselves of auto-suggestion in order to assist them in obtaining sound, restful sleep. A suggestion should be framed in such words as, "I'll sleep all night." "I started on the formula prescribed for putting you to sleep," stated a housewife, "and I was really amazed, for I had retired at night lying awake for hours with things going over in my mind time and time again. Now I can go to bed and fall fast asleep, with my mind so clear, knowing I am getting better."

Two alternatives to the repetition of a formula are suggested by the following remarks of one-time sufferers from insomnia. A Liverpool man says: "I find it easy to go to sleep if I think of the tapping of train wheels on rail-joints." A single 61-year-old dog breeder asserts: "I have been making my mind a blank for the last twenty years! I taught myself to do so in order to sleep and not lie awake with worry."

Besides ensuring that we sleep long enough, auto-suggestion may also be used to prevent our sleeping too long. If you have to get up at a certain hour and have no alarm-clock, you should suggest to yourself: "I'll wake at five," or "I'll wake at six", or whatever the hour is, and you will find that you will awaken at the time suggested.

"I have never used an alarm-clock," a married 28-year-old upholsterer informs us, "but have always decided the time that I should like to awaken by saying that time to myself about six times before going to sleep. I frequently vary the time of awakening but the method never fails me. I sleep late only when I fail to decide my time before sleeping."

CHAPTER IX

Sleep and Anxiety

IN the last chapter we discussed some ways and means of making sure that we obtain the maximum value from our sleep. No matter what advice we give, however, there will probably be some people who still fail to secure relief by any of these methods.

To these people we would repeat what we have already said: the quest of sleep by the insomniac is based upon the widespread belief that the lack of it is both abnormal and harmful. This belief is not only false, but is itself a cause of sleeplessness, since worry about loss of sleep will prevent sleep from coming. This assurance will offer them some consolation that will set their minds at rest.

The idea that everyone needs eight hours' sleep a day is a delusion. Actually, as we have seen, the older we get the less sleep we need, and when we are emotionally disturbed we may not sleep because then our need is to escape the anxiety that dreams provoke. This our insomnia permits us to do.

When sleep refuses to come, therefore, instead of lying in the dark, tossing and turning and brooding over the problems that press upon your consciousness, try this further suggestion. Get up and get busy. Most people complain that they lack the time to do all they would like to do. If you are one of these, the extra hours granted by sleeplessness may be used to do things in which you have always been interested, but for which you never quite found time.

If your sleepless nights are used in this way, they will lose their terror for you. You will cheerfully resign yourself to staying awake and will cease to worry about it. Thus relaxed in mind and body, you may suddenly discover that you have cured your insomnia. The absorption of your attention in something interesting will effectively relieve your worry, and you may even find yourself regretting the time that has to be given up to sleep.

One person who was formerly bothered by insomnia said: "I have learned to enjoy my insomnia by reading short stories. Before long I fall asleep."

TRY NOT TO SLEEP

For those who do not wish to go as far as this, here is a further suggestion that may appeal. Probably the harder you try to sleep, the wider awake you become. This is because you are attempting to use will-power to go to sleep, while in your imagination you picture yourself lying awake. Now when the imagination and the will come into conflict, the imagination always proves the stronger. The result is that you continue to lie awake.

The method that will help you to sleep is based upon the principle of trying *not* to sleep. A deliberate effort is made to stay awake. This is accompanied by the realization that you are doing it in order to overcome your sleeplessness. When you will yourself to stay awake, your imagination rebels and begins to picture how nice it would be to go to sleep. The outcome of the conflict between the will and the imagination is that the imagination wins. This makes it possible for you to go to sleep.

Therefore, when you get into bed, resolve that you will stay awake. Make a deliberate effort *not* to go to sleep. Say to yourself: "I am putting this method into practice in order to obtain sound sleep, and I realize that it is gradually being successful in helping me to do so." From time to time remind yourself that you are making a deliberate effort to stay awake in order to overcome your sleeplessness. This realization is most important. On no account should it be omitted.

The more you try to stay awake by this method, the sleepier you will find yourself becoming. By attempting to stay awake when you really want to sleep, you bring the will into conflict with the imagination. When this happens the imagination is always the victor. In spite of all your efforts to stay awake by will-power, the imagination, which pictures you sound asleep, will prove the stronger and actually give you the sleep you desire.

The psychological principle upon which this method is based is known as the law of reversed effort. This law is well illustrated not only by the application of the method, but also by the condition of the person who suffers from insomnia. When a person thinks, "I would like to do such-and-such a thing, but I do not think I can," he is unlikely to succeed by willing himself to do it.

No matter how much the insomniac wills himself to fall asleep, he believes that he cannot and so he remains awake. The harder he tries to go to sleep, the wider awake he becomes.

Instead of attempting to use will-power to overcome such a complaint as this, use should be made of imagination. If the person who suffers from insomnia can give up caring whether he sleeps or not, he should simply think to himself, "I am going to relax completely. As I relax my nerves are getting calm and peaceful. As they get calm and peaceful, I begin to feel tired. I am beginning to feel tired already, and the more I relax the more tired I become."

The auto-suggestions, by acting upon the imagination, avoid the operation of the law referred to above. A person who uses them will fall asleep before he hardly realizes what is happening to him.

Practical experience is always the proof of whether or not a method will work. The methods advocated up to this point have been put to the test of practical experience by former sufferers from insomnia. The following reports are sufficient proof that they have been found to work.

"I find the auto-suggestion exercise wonderful for sleeplessness; about a dozen repetitions and I am sound asleep," states a single 41-year-old porter.

A single 48-year-old clerical worker complained of insomnia, "which had been very bad." One month after being advised on these lines she stated: "My insomnia is reduced." Three weeks later her report was: "The insomnia has been cured."

A single 28-year-old miner suffered from insomnia and nervous trouble (lack of confidence, "bad nerves"). Within four months he had overcome both conditions. "I can now sleep," he affirmed, "after using auto-suggestion as prescribed." Even within one month he had reported: "I am sleeping better and getting more confident."

A 28-year-old shorthand typist complained of insomnia. Five months later she reported: "My insomnia is a thing of the past."

HIDDEN ANXIETY

It has been said in the previous chapter that in order to sleep well it is necessary to live a well-ordered life. Especially is it necessary to practise the much neglected art of moderation. It has been found that there is a certain connection between kidney trouble and insomnia. Cases of insomnia are often found among those who are in the habit of leading a gay life: for when the body is intoxicated by alcohol, the kidneys fail to function properly because they are overworked in eliminating the bodily poisons.

People who are immoderate in their habits of living are often victims of emotional maladjustment, which shows itself in other signs as well. These signs include not only the inability to get to sleep; when they do finally "drop off", their sleep may be haunted by terrifying dreams.

Where anxiety lies hidden from view it will eventually express itself in some way or other, and the disturbance of sleep is one of its favourite channels of expression. A frequent psychological cause of insomnia is a fear of sleep. Insomnia prevents the individual from coming face to face with the repressed desires which he would meet in his dreams. The avoidance of sleep permits him to run away from them.

A man who was troubled in this way stated: "Sometimes I even dread to sleep for fear that I might do these things, and so I have a sleepless night at times." The things in question were the murders that he committed in his dreams.

Although consciously he desires nothing so much as a good night's rest, the victim of insomnia may suffer from an unconscious phobia of falling asleep. He will ostensibly try to put himself to sleep by measures which in fact tend to keep him awake. The kind of sleep that he really wants is the dreamless sleep that he knew in early infancy. His phobia, however, springs from the fact that unconsciously he has associated sleep itself with dreams of anxiety and falling asleep with the thought of dying.

For example, a married 31-year-old man said: "I suddenly awake with a terrible feeling of anxiety. I even get the idea sometimes that I shall go to sleep and shan't awake again."

The relationship between insomnia and anxiety-dreams is seen

44

still more clearly in the case of a 45-year-old housewife. Staying awake enabled her to avoid what she described as "my two horrible dreams." In the first of these she was guilty of cannibalism. This shows incidentally that what the primitive savage performs in actuality survives as a fantasy in the mind of modern man. In the other she applied "a most disgusting name" to Jesus Christ.

In other words, this lady's insomnia was a defence against the anxiety provoked by her dreams of cannibalism and blasphemy. Under the circumstances we need not be surprised that she preferred to stay awake.

NATURE'S WARNING SIGNAL

We see then that if you cannot sleep without taking drugs, this may be Nature's signal that you do not need to sleep. It may mean that you have some other problem which you are unable or unwilling to recognize. Nature in her wisdom realizes that it is more important for you to solve this problem than it is to get eight hours' sleep. In any case, as previously indicated, the older you get after fifty the less sleep you normally require, even if you have no emotional problems to keep you awake.

Under these circumstances treatment to relieve the insomnia itself may be ineffectual, since this may not be the real problem but merely a sign of it. It would be better for such a person to examine his emotional adjustment to the demands of life as a whole and try to find out in what way it is breaking down.

If none of the methods prescribed hitherto brings relief to you, this probably means that your insomnia is a symptom of a serious nervous disorder, of which you display other symptoms as well. In this case you should consult a psychiatrist or psycho-analyst through your usual doctor, or a qualified non-medical psychologist or lay analyst privately, for the psychiatric treatment or psychotherapy which you need for your neurosis.

The fact that you dream is no cause for anxiety; indeed it would be odd if you did not dream. We all dream, although only some of us remember our dreams and none of us remembers all of them. The new scientific psychology teaches that, to quote the words of one of its ablest exponents, "...the best bedtime wish is not the old one of 'pleasant dreams', but rather the new scientific one of 'successful dreams'—dreams that will safeguard you against every disturbing irritation, both of the world around you as you sleep and the greater world stored up in your inner self."

Let us use the constructive truths of this science, and the common-sense laws of health, mental and physical, to secure for ourselves the benefits of sleep.

CHAPTER X

The Shadow of Coming Events

ACCORDING to the press, Mrs Winnie Banks, a 36-year-old Yorkshire housewife, dreamed in four years the winners of several classic races, although before she went to bed she did not know the names of the horses entered for them. Before she began to have these dreams she had no interest in racehorses and had never made a bet.

She dreamed the name of a winner starting with "A". The next day she spotted Airborne in the list of runners. She dreamed that she was on holiday at Cloncarrig, although she had never been to Ireland. A horse of this name won the Grand National. In the case of Sheila's Cottage, another Grand National winner, she dreamed of the jockey's colours, black and white. She dreamed that she was calling to her baby, "Come here, my love." The next day My Love won the Derby.

"All that I am now going to write of," stated a man, "is perfectly true. I seldom ever bet on horses, but my family do, and naturally I hear plenty of talk of horses and big races. Anyway, on the eve of this year's Lincoln (1948) I fell asleep thinking of the race. I had a dream and it was very distinct.

"I remember standing at a bar at the racecourse. Over a loud speaker I heard a voice distinctly announce as the winner number six, second number five. I repeated the numbers several times. Then I awoke. I repeated the dream at the breakfast table, and we counted the horses down in the morning paper. That afternoon the sixth horse that we had counted won the Lincoln and the fifth was second. We found out afterwards that the saddle-cloth on the winner was number six and on the second number five. I recounted the dream several times at home that morning before the race, as it was very vivid.

"Only one person in the family of five backed the winner on account of this dream. How we have wished since that we had taken notice of the dream! Five adults are witnesses that I told the dream time after time before the race."

A housewife said that one of her daughters had what she called "the same uncanny gift". This daughter predicted that Newcastle United would win the F.A. Cup in 1951, because she had seen their victory occur in a dream. The dream was related on the morning of the day that the game was played. "She knows nothing at all about football," her mother added, "and is not a bit interested in it." The mother herself had also had dreams about a certain horse winning a big race or a certain team winning the Cup. "At the time I was not at all interested," she declared, "in either horse-racing or football and knew nothing about them."

On the morning of Derby day, 1933, a man dreamed that he heard the names of the first two winners announced. He was so impressed that, although not normally interested in racing, he listened to the broadcast of the race and was surprised to find that his dream was correct.

"Some years ago on the night before the big race," said a 49-year-old bricklayer, "I saw in my dream the horses passing the winning-post and heard their names called out. I wrote down the names of the first three horses at the breakfast table. My premonition was correct. I do not take any interest in horse-racing and I never bet on horses."

Not all allegedly predictive dreams come true. For example, a national daily newspaper announced that its tipster "saw" the "winner" of the 1951 Manchester November Handicap in a dream a fortnight before the race was run. The horse in question was the favourite, Western Window, which in the dream won the race by half a length. Western Window was placed eighth in the actual race, and no further reference to the dream appeared in the newspaper.

The same newspaper published a letter from a Mrs M. Walls of London, who wrote reporting a dream that the Coronation Stone, stolen from Westminster Abbey, was in Southend. She stated that her dream also contained a reference to the name of Hutton and a hill. As everyone knows, when the Coronation Stone was eventually restored, none of these references had any bearing on the matter.

WHAT HAPPENED AT 3.45

The housewife mentioned above also described the following dream:

"I glanced at the clock and saw it was 3.45. Just then I heard a loud knock on the front door. On opening the door I saw a man standing on the step. He was tall and broad, wore a check cap and a mackintosh, and had what I took to be a large 'tummy'. He asked me if ———— (my husband's name) lived here. I answered 'Yes'; he then handed me a paper and asked: 'Will you give him that?' With these words in my ears I awoke."

What actually happened next day was described by the lady as follows: "I was busy about the house and just happened to glance at the clock. It was 3.45. Just then a loud knock came at the front door. On opening the door, to my amazement I saw the man in my dream standing there. It gave me quite a shock. He was identical in every way, except that what I took to be a large 'tummy' in my dream turned out to be his arm under his mac, evidently in a sling. He asked me the same questions and handed me a paper to give to my husband. It was a summons to serve on a jury."

The dreamer asked, as the reader will ask: "How can one explain dreams like these?" She added: "It is only one of many that I have had. They are too numerous to write down."

A 29-year-old housewife said that on one occasion she dreamed that her girl-friend had a baby girl, and she actually saw it born in her dream. "My distinct memory of it," she wrote, "was of large blue eyes. I wrote and told my friend, who wrote back and said she *was* expecting a baby. When the baby came, it was a girl with large blue eyes. Was this because I wanted this to happen to my friend?"

A predictive dream was recorded by Charles Dickens in 1863. He writes: "I dreamt that I saw a lady in a red shawl with her back to me (whom I supposed to be E.). On her turning round, I found that I didn't know her, and she said, 'I am Miss Napier'." Dickens confesses that he had never heard of a Miss Napier. This dream occurred on a Thursday night. On the Friday night he was visited by two friends who brought with them a lady in a red shawl. Her name turned out to be Miss Napier.

In 1902 Dr W. F. Prince, President of the Society for Psychical Research, dreamed that he was looking at a train, the rear end of which was protruding from a railway tunnel. Then, suddenly, another train dashed into it. He saw the coaches crumple and pile up, and out of the mass of wreckage came screams from the wounded. Next morning an express, while standing with its rear end at the entrance of the Park Avenue tunnel in New York City, was struck by the engine of a local train. The advancing locomotive ploughed into the standing train, smashing the coaches and killing and wounding many of the passengers.

Another classical example of an apparently predictive dream is associated with the loss of the *Titanic*. The ship was due to sail on her maiden voyage on April 10th, 1912. On or about March 23rd a Mr Middleton booked his passage. Some days later he dreamed that he saw the huge vessel floating on the sea keel upwards and her passengers and crew swimming around. On the following night the dream occurred again. At first the dreamer was reluctant to cancel his passage, but on April 4th he received a cablegram which gave him an excuse for doing so. This was in spite of the fact that everyone had said that the new liner was "unsinkable". The *Titanic* left Southampton on April 10th, and was wrecked on the night of April 14th-15th.

THE PRESIDENT'S DREAM

One of the most celebrated examples of a predictive dream was experienced by Abraham Lincoln, who dreamed in advance of his own death. A few days before his assassination he had this dream: "Before me was a catafalque on which rested a corpse wrapped in funeral vestments. Around it were stationed soldiers who were acting as guards. 'Who is dead in the White House?' I demanded of one of the soldiers. 'The President,' was the answer; 'he was killed by an assassin!' "

On the night that Lincoln fell to the assassin's bullet and the news was broken to Mrs Lincoln, her first words were: "His dream was prophetic!" His body lay in state in the White House, with a guard of soldiers about it, precisely as he had seen it in that strange prevision. What explanation are we to give?

Do dreams predict the future? Before we can answer this question, we must establish the facts. There is little point in discussing it unless we are sure that apparently predictive dreams do occur. In view of the examples that we have brought forward, we need no longer remain in uncertainty on this particular point.

We have been content so far to accept the genuineness of so-called predictive dreams. The weight of evidence that we have presented cannot lightly be set on one side. What the explanation of such dreams may be is a further problem that we have still to settle.

A body of evidence is gradually accumulating to show that a minority of dreams may predict the future. In every case, however, one should explore what connection they may have with the past before assuming a predictive element in them. I think that some so-called "predictive" dreams really relate to the past, and some, perhaps, relate both to the past and to the future, since what happens in the future is the outcome of what is taking place now and what has taken place in the past.

Dr Alfred Adler, the founder of Individual Psychology, regarded the dream in a different light from Freud. He saw it not as a fulfilment of past wishes, but as a rehearsal of future actions. According to him, dreams reflect current and future unsolved problems and rehearse their possible solutions. It cannot, however, be claimed that Adler said that dreams actually predict what will take place in the future.

Dr C. G. Jung, who like Adler was formerly a disciple of Freud, believes that dreams may have several meanings. They may be, as Freud considered, an expression of repressed wishes of the past, or, as Adler held, a foreshadowing of things to come, or, on the other hand, a manifestation of present conflict. Jung tends to favour the last-mentioned view. A patient's dreams he interprets not simply as revealing old repressed sex wishes, but as indicating the patient's unconscious attitude towards his present problem.

The chief difficulty that has no doubt deterred psychologists from the study and investigation of predictive dreams is that the problem bristles with puzzling philosophical implications. If the future can be predicted in dreams, then in some incomprehensible way it must already exist. But if the future already exists, what becomes of free will? It may well be that the concept of free will will have to be abandoned as an illusion arising out of our imperfect comprehension of the nature of time.

This is a view towards which psychological determinism leans. This doctrine holds that all our actions are determined by definite causes. The feeling of free will arises out of the capacity of the conscious mind to observe its own operation. Of the many conflicting impulses that strive for supremacy in our minds, the one that succeeds in winning it is conceived as our free will. What we perceive, however, is only a small part of what actually occurs in our mind. "Of course," remarked the late Dr A. A. Brill, "there is no such thing (as free will) in psychiatry or in the natural sciences. Everything must be determined."

The general position seems to be this: we should examine a dream for its relation to the past before we declare that it predicts the future, but to attempt to relate them to the past does not exhaust the possibilities in all dreams. There are certain dreams that seem to compel us to assume that they have some bearing on the future, if we are to explain them properly. The whole matter is debatable, however, and such a statement as this might well be attacked as either too conservative or too speculative.

CHAPTER XI

Other Views about Dreams

AS we have seen, there is a vast region of the mind below the level of consciousness, in which painful memories and unfulfilled wishes are kept in a state of repression, and from which they emerge to manifest themselves in dreams as well as in many other ways.

This theory has been developed and modified by Adler and Jung, to whom we referred in chapter X. Both the Individual Psychology of Adler and the analytical psychology of Jung are based upon the doctrine of the unconscious. The result is that there are now several different schools of thought in existence.

Adler sees the dream not as a fulfilment of past wishes, but as a rehearsal of future actions. It is important to the psychologist because it reveals the individual's fundamental attitude to his problems.

Adler's view may be illustrated by means of the dream in which the individual finds himself back at school, about to take an examination which in reality he passed years ago. According to the Individual Psychologist, this dream may have one meaning for one dreamer and a different one for another dreamer. Depending upon the nature of the dreamer's problems, a knowledge of which is required for a satisfactory interpretation, the meaning to be given to the dream will vary. For one dreamer it may mean, "I am not prepared to face the problem before me." For another dreamer it may mean, "I have passed this examination before and I will pass the test before me at present."

For Adler the most important step in understanding dreams was the discovery of what he called the dreamer's "style of life". The purpose of the dream he regarded as that of exciting "the mood in which we are prepared to meet the situation."

FOUR FUNCTIONS

Jung holds that the mind has four basic functions that are present in every individual. These are thought, feeling, sensation and intuition. The thought function may be called the intellectual; the feeling function may be called the emotional; the sensation function the physical; and the intuition function the imaginative.

Thought seeks to understand the world on the basis of a "true-false" evaluation; feeling apprehends it on the basis of a "pleasant-unpleasant" evaluation. Sensation perceives things through the senses; intuition is an inner perception of the potentialities in things. The two pairs of opposites, thought-feeling and sensation-intuition, are compensatory of each other. The goal of the individual in Jungian psychology is a state of "wholeness", in which all four functions are at the individual's command in as nearly the same degree as possible. In other words, he seeks an all-round well-developed personality.

Instead of one unconscious, Jung has two—a personal and a collective unconscious. The personal unconscious is those contents of the unconscious which can be raised into consciousness. The collective unconscious results from the inherited brain structure of the individual and is common to all humanity. It consists of primitive ways of thinking which manifest themselves in dreams, in the night terrors of children, in the ravings of the insane. Father, mother, child, male and female, generation, growth and decay are primitive facts which have impressed themselves on racial thought. The study of mythology as well as of dreams is invaluable for the light which it throws on the collective unconscious.

Here is a dream that seems to lend itself to interpretation on Jungian lines. A young man reported that he dreamed of four beautiful gardens which he had never actually seen before. They were placed side by side. On the extreme left was an unfinished sunken garden which he was completing; next a bed of roses and flowering shrubs. This was followed by a bed of flowers, and on the extreme right there was a paved garden with flowers and plants in tubs. He added that the gardens were not owned by anyone he knew.

54

It is tempting to identify the four gardens which figure in this dream with the four functions of the dreamer's personality, according to the Jungian scheme. He had never seen the gardens before, nor were they owned by anyone he knew. In other words, he was not fully aware of the qualities of his own personality and did not know that he possessed them. The flowers in the gardens are the hidden treasures of the collective unconscious.

The four gardens differ from one another just as no two functions of an individual's personality are alike. One function of the dreamer's personality is incomplete and submerged, as symbolized by the unfinished sunken garden. He knows less about this part of his real self than he does about the other parts. The fact that in his dream the dreamer is engaged in working in this sunken garden shows that he is aware of his deficiencies and wishes to remedy them. The dream shows the dreamer striving to achieve "wholeness".

A COMPARISON

Summing up the differences between Freud, Adler and Jung in the matter of dream interpretation, Robert S. Woodworth says: "Jung has contrasted his own and the Freudian interpretations in the instance of a dream of a young man, recently graduated from the university, who had been unable to settle on an occupation and had fallen into a neurosis. The dream was:

"I was going up a flight of stairs with my mother and sister. When we reached the top I was told that my sister was soon to have a child."

"This would be easy for a Freudian," continues Professor Woodworth, "climbing stairs being accepted as a regular symbol for sex activity, and the mother and sister being the regular objects of the infantile incest desires. The dream would be clearly a fulfilment of a repressed infantile wish. Not satisfied with this ready interpretation Jung proceeded to obtain free associations starting from each element of the dream.

"The mother suggested neglect of his duties, since he had long neglected his mother. The sister suggested true love for a woman. Climbing the stairs suggested making a success of life, and the prospective baby suggested new birth or regeneration for himself. Jung concluded that the dream revealed the stirring of unconscious energies toward meeting the young man's present situation."

Jung criticizes the Freudian interpretation on the ground that certain parts of the manifest content are taken symbolically, while others are taken literally. Climbing the stairs, for instance, is interpreted as a symbol, but the mother and sister stand for themselves. "By what method can we determine," asks Jung, "whether a particular part is to be taken symbolically or literally?" In other words, his criticism amounts to a charge of inconsistency, which he avoids himself by treating all elements in the manifest content as symbols.

How Adler, who believed that the individual's position in the family was important, would interpret this dream we cannot tell, lacking information as to whether the dreamer was the oldest child or younger than his sister.

Although he did not mean that a person's style of life was governed merely by his order in the family, Adler held that the eldest child tends to adopt a conservative attitude, while the second child, on the other hand, develops the attitude of striving to excel. The youngest child may be the spoilt darling of the family. The only child may become tyrannical. It appears that there is no position in the family which is not fraught with its own peculiar dangers from the point of view of its effect on the emotional development of the individual.

Professor Woodworth suggests that it should not be difficult for the Individual Psychologist to "see a dependent style of life in this dream, since the dreamer did not climb the stairs alone."

As he goes on to point out, the fact that several divergent interpretations can be made of the same dream may make one doubt the validity of any dream interpretation. This is not as serious a criticism as it appears at first sight, for if the dream-mind is as versatile as we believe it to be, a dream ought to be capable of several interpretations.

Jung is even prepared to admit that he is not too concerned about whether a dream interpretation is "true" in the scientific sense. He considers that the welfare of the dreamer is more important than the truth of the interpretation. The real test, in his opinion, is: "Does the interpretation help the dreamer to 'sort himself out'?" If this is accomplished, the interpretation has served its purpose. This is a point of view with which we can immediately sympathize.

CHAPTER XII

Dreams in the Bible

BESIDES the wealth of theology, history, poetry, folklore, prophecy, law and ethics which the Bible contains, it also lays claim to rank highly as an important source of dreams and their interpretations.

The dreams recorded in the pages of Holy Scripture are valuable for two reasons. In the first place they show that the dream-mind speaks the same language in different races and at different times.

Although the ancient peoples attached importance to dreams as omens and guides to future conduct—even as predictions of the future—we may nevertheless trace the wishes that their dreams attempted to fulfil. Thus we are provided with illustrations of the modern view that dreams are related to the wishes which the dreamer has harboured in the past, but which for some reason have failed to be gratified in waking life.

In this way we are led to realize that human nature is essentially the same in all epochs and in all nations, for the thoughts and aims that we find reflected in biblical dreams have much in common with those of to-day.

"The dreams of someone living to-day in New York or in Paris," remarks Dr Erich Fromm, "are the same as the dreams reported from people living some thousand years ago in Athens or in Jerusalem."

The dream that Pilate's wife communicated to her husband might be one told by any anxious wife of modern times to a husband confronted with an important matter involving another person and calling for a fair decision vitally affecting that person's welfare.

The dream that Gideon overheard a Midianite soldier recounting to his comrade might be a dream told by a modern serviceman to an army psychiatrist. The wish that is revealed in it could have been harboured under similar circumstances by any victim of "battle fatigue" in to-day's warfare.

Secondly, the dreams of the Bible are important because they give us an insight into the minds and characters of men and women who distinguished themselves in other ways apart from their fertility in dreaming or their skill in interpreting dreams. The dreams that are associated with the name of Joseph commend themselves to us for their importance from this point of view. For this reason we may use them as a help in understanding the motives that drove these men to action.

Let us consider the dreams to which we have referred in connection with the first point, and then the dreams that Joseph interpreted or had himself.

Pilate's wife, we are told, sent a message to him as he was seated in the place of judgment and advised him in respect of Jesus: "Have thou nothing to do with that just man: for I have suffered many things this day in a dream because of him." (Matthew 27, 19.) The dream reflects the dreamer's wish to punish herself in order to atone for her sense of guilt in relation to the treatment that had been meted out to Jesus.

Before his battle with the Midianites, Gideon, the commander-in-chief of the forces of Israel, overheard a Midianite soldier recounting a dream to his comrade.

The dream is recorded in Judges 7, 13 in the following words: "A cake of barley bread tumbled into the host of Midian, and came unto a tent, and smote it that it fell, and overturned it, that the tent lay along."

The soldier's comrade offered the following interpretation: "This is nothing else save the sword of Gideon the son of Joash, a man of Israel: for into his hand hath God delivered Midian, and all the host." (Judges 7, 14.) This implies that the dream may be taken as reflecting the Midianite dreamer's wish that the Israelites should be victorious in the coming conflict.

This view is supported by our observation of the poor morale of the Midianite host, who fled without offering any resistance when Gideon and a mere three hundred men entered their camp.

FAMINE AND PLENTY

Two dreams of Pharaoh are recorded in Genesis 41. In the first we are told that Pharaoh "stood by the river. And, behold, there came up out of the river seven well favoured kine and fatfleshed; and they fed in a meadow. And, behold, seven other kine came up after them out of the river, ill favoured and leanfleshed; and stood by the other kine upon the brink of the river. And the ill favoured and leanfleshed kine did eat up the seven well favoured and fat kine."

This dream was repeated in another version, which differs in the manifest content, although the latent content was shown by Joseph to be the same.

In the second dream "seven ears of corn came up upon one stalk, rank and good. And, behold, seven thin ears and blasted with the east wind sprung up after them. And the seven thin ears devoured the seven rank and full ears."

In interpreting the two dreams, Joseph treated them as a single dream. "The seven good kine," he said, "are seven years; and the seven good ears are seven years." To the seven lean cattle and the seven empty ears he gave the meaning of seven years of famine.

"There come seven years of great plenty throughout all the land of Egypt," continued Joseph. "And there shall arise after them seven years of famine; and all the plenty shall be forgotten in the land of Egypt; and the famine shall consume the land."

Can these dreams and their interpretation be brought into line with the wish-fulfilment theory? To do this, we must suppose that Pharaoh unconsciously wished for seven years of plenty and seven years of famine. The fact that Joseph's interpretation told him what he had unconsciously wanted to hear, might explain why he rewarded Joseph so handsomely by setting him next to himself as ruler over Egypt.

Pharaoh's motive for desiring seven lean years is more obscure. Perhaps he already intended to do what Joseph later advised, *i.e.*, to store grain in the years of plenty against the possibility of famine. This would reflect credit upon himself and mitigate the danger of unrest among the people. He may have hoped that he would benefit by selling grain to his own people and to other countries, as indeed subsequently proved to be the case.

That it was not unknown to expect a famine to last for seven years may be observed from II Kings 8, 1, where we read that Elisha predicted a famine lasting for the same period of time.

Besides the dreams of Pharaoh, Joseph also interpreted those of Pharaoh's butler and baker, whom he met while in prison. The butler's dream was as follows: "A vine was before me; and in the vine were three branches: and it was as though it budded, and her blossoms shot forth; and the clusters thereof brought forth ripe grapes: and Pharaoh's cup was in my hand: and I took the grapes, and pressed them into Pharaoh's cup, and I gave the cup into Pharaoh's hand." (Genesis 40, 9-11.)

Joseph's interpretation was that the three branches stood for three days, within which the butler would regain his master's favour. He would then be restored to his former position, in which he would hand Pharaoh his cup as he did in the dream.

On his birthday, which fell three days later, Pharaoh could be expected to make some show of magnanimity, just as Herod on his own birthday promised the daughter of Herodias anything she asked. (Matthew 14, 7.) The butler wished that he might profit on this occasion by being given his freedom and restored to office, when he would hand Pharaoh his cup, just as we are told that Nehemiah did for King Artaxerxes. (Nehemiah 2, 1.) Joseph's acute powers of observation must have divined this motive at work in the mind of the butler and he interpreted the latter's dream in accordance with it.

THE BAKER'S DREAM

The baker's dream was as follows: "I had three white baskets on my head: and in the uppermost basket there was of all manner of bakemeats for Pharaoh; and the birds did eat them out of the basket upon my head." (Genesis 40, 16-17.) Joseph interpreted the three baskets as representing three days, within which Pharaoh would hang the baker and the birds would eat his flesh.

Joseph interpreted the butler's dream correctly as expressing his wish to be liberated on Pharaoh's birthday, and be restored to the service of his master. Why did he not conclude that the baker, too, wished to regain his position? If Joseph's interpretation was correct, are we justified in inferring that the baker's dream expressed a wish to be hanged within three days?

One point we notice about the baker's dream is that although the bakemeats were intended for Pharaoh, the birds received them instead. May we not assume that the baker wished him to have the bakemeats in order to influence Pharaoh in his favour? He may also have wished him not to have the bakemeats in revenge for the treatment he had received at Pharaoh's hands. If the baker's hostility to his royal master was enough to compel his subsequent execution, may he not have felt guilty about it and sought to atone for it by imagining his own death in symbolic form in his dream?

One of Joseph's own dreams to be found in Genesis 37, 5-8 is: "We were binding sheaves in the field, and, lo, my sheaf arose, and also stood upright; and, behold, your sheaves stood round about, and made obeisance to my sheaf." We are told that Joseph's brothers hated him all the more when they realized the vaunting ambition revealed in the dream.

"Shalt thou indeed reign over us?" they asked him. "Or shalt thou indeed have dominion over us?"

Joseph is an outstanding example of the character of a man who was psychologically both the youngest and favourite son of his father and the only son of his mother. Jacob's first wife, Leah, and his wives' handmaids were the mothers of Joseph's brothers and sister, whereas Joseph's mother was Jacob's second wife, Rachel.

It is true that Joseph's mother died in giving birth to his younger brother, Benjamin, but having left the family circle, Joseph remained psychologically in the position of the youngest son. We learn from Genesis 37, 3 that Jacob "loved Joseph more than all his children, because he was the son of his old age."

Joseph's dream of his brothers' sheaves of corn bowing down before his own sheaf shows the striving of the youngest son, encouraged by his father's favouritism and his monopoly of his mother's affection, to excel the whole family, whose hostility towards him also acted as an incentive to his urge to attain a position of power and superiority.

Lewis Way in *Adler's Place in Psychology* refers to "the peculiarly gracious and social form that such a striving can take. Although the ears of corn of his father and brothers must bow before his ear, yet the corn itself is a symbol of his desire to excel by becoming more fruitful than they, a dream that he was later to fulfil when he saved the land of Egypt from famine."

"In his dream," writes Dr Erich Fromm in *The Forgotten Language*, "he is more closely aware of his extraordinary gifts than he could be in his waking life, where he was impressed by the fact that he was younger and weaker than all his brothers. His dream is a blend of his passionate ambition and an insight into his gifts without which his dream could not have come true."

"No better example of early dream interpretation can be found than the story of Joseph in the book of Genesis," writes William Oliver Stevens in *The Mystery of Dreams*. And, it might be added, none which more clearly illustrates the modern theory of dreams as the disguised fulfilment of a wish which has been entertained in the mind of the dreamer, but denied actual fulfilment in waking life.

CHAPTER XIII

The Eternal Triangle in Dreams

THE psychology of the unconscious was the first science to trace human behaviour and experience, including dreams, back to early childhood. Our ideas about what makes us act the way that we do have been revolutionized by the findings which it has made known. Prominent among these findings is the view that the psycho-sexual life of the individual does not begin at puberty, but at birth.

The child's first relationship is with the mother or her substitute. Since she is the earliest on the scene, it is not surprising that her influence should be the most lasting. Since the earliest days of recorded history there has been a general recognition that the function of motherhood largely determines the character of the human race.

The child later becomes aware of the existence of his father, who also plays an important part in the unfolding of his love-life. We learn from the study of the psychology of the unconscious that the male child early on forms an unconscious attachment to his mother, coupled with an unconscious hostility against his father, whom he not only admires and respects but in whom he sees a rival for the love of his mother.

It would be nearer the truth to say that this important fact was rediscovered in modern times, for it was almost certainly known to the ancient Greeks, as their mythology shows. The legend of Oedipus tells how an oracle foretold that Laïus, King of Thebes, would die at the hand of his son. When his son, Oedipus, was born, Laïus caused him to be exposed on Mount Cithaeron, where he was discovered by a herdsman and taken to Polybus, King of Corinth, to be brought up as his own son.

Oedipus, being told by the oracle at Delphi that he was destined to slay his father and marry his mother, did not return to Corinth, but proceeded to Thebes to escape the fate predicted for him. As he approached Thebes he met a chariot carrying his real father, whom, of course, he did not recognize. Being ordered out of the way by the charioteer, he got into an argument, in the course of which he came to blows with Laïus and killed him.

THE RIDDLE OF THE SPHINX

In the meantime the famous Sphinx had appeared near Thebes and was terrorising the city. This monster propounded a riddle to everyone who passed by, putting to death all who failed to solve it. The riddle of the Sphinx was: "What is it that goes first on four legs, then on two, and finally on three?"

The people of Thebes offered a reward of the kingdom and the hand of the Queen to whoever should deliver them from the monster. Oedipus solved the riddle of the Sphinx by answering correctly: "Man, because as an infant he crawls on all fours, as an adult he walks upright, and in old age he walks with the aid of a stick."

Oedipus received the reward, becoming king in his real father's place and marrying his mother, Queen Jocasta. When he discovered the identity of his wife, he symbolically emasculated himself by putting out his own eyes, while Queen Jocasta hanged herself.

The Oedipus complex, which is named after this Greek legend, is the male child's unconscious attachment to his mother, coupled with unconscious love of and hostility against his father, whom he sees as a rival for the love of the former.

A complex is a system of repressed ideas dominated by some emotion. Such a mental system is like a foreign body in the mind —a part of the unconscious mind, influencing consciousness without revealing itself in its true form. It may be thought of as producing mental strain and giving rise to all sorts of "kinks" and "quirks" of behaviour.

The formation of the Oedipus complex is the most significant emotional occurrence of the years of childhood, and upon its handling depends much of the individual's subsequent happiness. Yet it is so completely forgotten or repressed that most of us are unaware of its existence, and are inclined to be sceptical when our attention is called to it. The fact remains, however, that in countless ways it makes its presence felt in later life.

For example, a husband with a son nearly twelve years old stated: "Our child tries to cause me to quarrel with my wife in the hope that I shall not live with her, so that he may have full attention and petting from her like a child half his age. This rather bothers me; I am not sure how to handle it, as I do not live a great deal with my wife."

A clear picture of the Oedipus situation may be gained from this report, which presents the struggle between father and son for the love of the mother.

In the case of the female child the roles of the mother and father are reversed. An analogous situation in Greek mythology has given rise to the term, "Electra complex". This complex takes its name from the myth of Electra, whose father, Agamemnon, was murdered by her mother, Clytemnestra. Later Electra helped her brother, Orestes, to avenge her father's death by slaying her mother.

The Electra complex is for women analogous to the Oedipus complex in men, so much so indeed that the latter term is generally used to describe both situations. For the sake of simplicity, therefore, we will refer to the early emotional situation of both the boy and the girl as the Oedipus complex, as this is justified by common usage.

We should not be surprised to find that the Oedipus conflict plays a prominent part in dreams.

For example, a single man of twenty-eight reported: "I dreamed of my mother as a young girl keeping company with me."

"It has a special significance for me," he added. Asked what the significance was, he replied: "My father died when I was ten years old, leaving my mother a young attractive widow. I was called up for the army when I was nineteen. In my periods of leave it used to be a joy for me to take mother out to lunch and a film matinée. That period was the beginning of a long, closely devoted loving friendship between my mother and me.

"Over a period of years my mother and I were gradually brought into a friendship that seldom exists between mother and son."

Here is another example:

"I was responsible for the distribution of a number of desk diaries at the office, and I had put half a dozen on one side. I went to the cupboard, took them out, and found that they had magically turned into six booklets entitled 'How to Take Care of a Baby'. I was faced with the task of distributing these booklets to the heads of departments, and saw nothing amusing in the situation."

In this dream the department heads, who are of superior status to the dreamer, are symbols of her father. By giving them the booklets she is inviting them to "take care of a baby" for her. In her sleep she is acting out the little girl's fantasy of having a child by her father.

RIVALS

The Oedipus complex frequently occurs as a motif in myths and dreams in the form of a fight between father and son. This is the form that it takes in the following dream reported by a single 24-year-old radio engineer:

"I was in a cathedral amongst a lot of tombs with marble effigies lying on top and nearby was a pile of swords. Suddenly a man appeared, dressed as in Saxon times with a helmet with horns on it. This man was twice normal size and he carried a sword, also twice normal size, which he swung at me. I dodged back and managed to pick up a sword from the pile, and thus ward off the blows whilst looking for an escape."

The cathedral in which the dreamer finds himself is probably a mother-symbol, since we are accustomed to speak of "Mother Church", while many churches are named after the Holy Mother. The man who appears dressed in a Saxon helmet is probably a father-figure, his size being mentioned in order to emphasize the difference in stature between parent and child, and to inform us that the dream deals with childhood matters.

In the dreams of women the rivalry between mother and daughter may take an equally violent form, as we may observe from the following dream recounted by a 24-year-old shorthand-typist.

"One night I had a dream in which my mother was hitting me on the head with an axe."

In other dreams the conflict between father and son appears under the guise of a race between two runners, either human or animal. For example, a young man dreamed of a race in which two horses were competing for the lead. When we refer to a mannish woman as "horsy", we testify to the role of a horse as a male symbol.

The horse which finally won the race in the young man's dream was called "Twenty Twenty". When on the following morning the young man consulted the list of runners at a race-meeting to be held that day, he found that a horse of this name was entered for one of the races. If the horse had won the race (which it did not), this dream would undoubtedly have been adduced as evidence in support of the view that some dreams predict the future.

The young man whose dream is quoted above also had another in which he himself was running round a track hard on the heels of another runner. In order that we may properly understand this dream, too, it is necessary that we should relate it to the motif of rivalry between son and father. The Oedipus situation was repeated in the second dream in the form of an attempt on the part of the dreamer (son) to catch up someone running in front of him (father).

In the first (horse-race) dream the dreamer was standing to the left of a jump and the race was run on a left-hand course. In the second dream he was running in a left-hand direction along the right-hand side of the oval track. The employment of this symbolism implies an act of moral judgment on the wish disguised by the dream. Right and left are to be understood in a moral sense, *i.e.*, right and wrong.

It would be a mistake to think that the Oedipus complex is found only in dreams. It makes itself felt in many other aspects of human affairs. To conclude this brief survey by quoting but one minor example, it explains the popularity of the literary theme of the eternal triangle. We intuitively realize its closeness to human experience, because each one of us has had to come to terms with it in early life. The spectacle of two men contending for the love of a woman appeals to us because it reawakens our own experience of the son-father-mother relationship. Although slightly less familiar, that of two women as rivals for the love of a man re-echoes the infantile daughter-mother-father situation.

The above remarks do not exhaust this important discovery of modern psychology, but at least enough has been said to illustrate the part that it plays in dreams.

CHAPTER XIV

Symbolism in Dreams

THE mental images experienced during sleep may clothe repressed wishes in symbolic guise. Symbolism means that an idea or process represents an associated one that is repressed in the unconscious, *e.g.*, a house may be a symbol of the human body. The use of symbolic language is already familiar to us in poetry. Dr Erich Fromm calls it "the one universal language the human race has ever developed, the same for all cultures and throughout history". Dr Jones tells us that "it is known that identical symbolisms occur in different parts of the world, and in different ages, in circumstances that preclude the possibility of their having been merely transplanted from one place to another."

"There appears to be a general tendency of the human mind," he continues, "to symbolize objects and interests of paramount and universal significance in forms that are psychologically the most suitable and available." It need not surprise us, therefore, to note the important part that symbols play in dreams.

A feature of symbolism is that while the number of objects that can act as symbols is unlimited, the number of ideas that they can symbolize is very few. These ideas are a mere handful closely related to the basic facts of human experience, such as birth, love, death, the members of one's immediate family circle, the human body and its various organs and parts. Only about half a dozen unconscious ideas are represented by countless numbers of symbols, of which we shall not have space to mention more than the most important ones.

As regards the application of symbolism to dreams, psychoanalysis tells us that where certain universal symbols appear, this may make it possible for us to dispense with the dreamer's associations. That is to say, we may be able to interpret the dream without the aid of the thoughts and memories that are associated with it in the dreamer's mind. Ordinarily we require him to produce these thoughts and memories, for they contain the meaning of the dream.

As Freud himself says: "In general we are not in a position to interpret the dream of another person if he is unwilling to furnish us with the unconscious thoughts which lie behind the dream content." A footnote, however, adds: "An exception is furnished by those cases in which the dreamer utilizes in the expression of his latent dream thoughts the symbols which are familiar to us."

MAN-MADE OBJECTS

According to Freud, the overwhelming majority of dream-symbols are sexual in nature. These are naturally of two kinds: male and female. In general, male symbols are long and pointed in shape, while female ones are rounded and hollow.

Examples of the former kind are aeroplanes, motor-cars, fire-arms, implements, keys, knives, cigarettes, sticks, umbrellas, poles, trees, pencils, sausages, weapons and tools. Objects that may stand as female symbols are boxes, cups, shoes, slippers, cupboards, ovens, stoves, rooms, drawers, chests, horseshoes, pits, caves, jars, bottles, pockets, purses and ships.

If we wish to observe the association between shoes and the female, we may remind ourselves of the nursery rhyme about the old woman who lived in a shoe. We are told that in a certain part of Germany people say of a woman who has had a child that "her oven has fallen to pieces". The use of ships as female symbols is echoed by the words of the New Testament, which refers to the woman as "the weaker vessel". (I Peter 3, 7.)

Also capable of acting as female symbols are balconies, window-sills, and projecting ledges, which symbolize the bosom. For instance, a young soldier dreamed that he was on the face of a high cliff, standing on a ledge. The symbolism of the dream disguised a repressed wish to return to the dependent position of the infant clinging to his mother's bosom. Since the dreamer did not like the army, we may infer that the dream sought to compensate him for his sense of insecurity.

Women are further represented in dreams by means of tables

and boards. The principle of association by contrast no doubt operates here, since tables and boards have no projecting contours. Closely associated with the ideas of table and board is the action of eating, which in dreams symbolizes marriage.

The principle of association by contrast may also be observed in the symbolic representation of nudity by means of clothes and uniforms. A cloak in a woman's dream stands for a man. We learn that among the bedouin the bridegroom covers the bride with a special cloak as part of their ancient marriage ceremony. References to similar practices among the Hebrews occur in the Bible. (See Ezekiel 16, 8 and Ruth 3, 9.)

A room came to be a female symbol because like the female it is capable of holding a human being. The room would also lend itself to this symbolism on account of the association between woman and the place reserved for her work.

A beloved person may be symbolized in a dream by a jewel or treasure, while the pleasures of love may be disguised as sweetmeats (*cf.* sweetheart). Materials such as wood and paper and objects made from them, *e.g.*, books, stand for women, as do towns, citadels, castles and fortresses.

Other symbols with a sexual meaning are buildings, stairs, doors, ladders, overcoats, hats, neckties, machinery, "lucky charms", luggage, milk, railway stations, department stores, roads and tunnels.

NATURAL OBJECTS

In addition to the man-made objects noted above, natural objects are employed by the unconscious mind for symbolic purposes. Male symbols that come under this heading are mountains, rocks, and the branches of trees. Female ones include flowers, fruit, the moon, hollow trees, gardens, islands, landscapes (especially with woods and expanses of water) and valleys. The Song of Solomon reminds us of this symbolism when it says: "A garden inclosed is my sister, my spouse; a spring shut up, a fountain sealed." (Song of Solomon 4, 12.)

"The lotus flower is an ancient divine symbol in India,"

records Paramhansa Yogananda in *Autobiography of a Yogi*; "its unfolding petals suggest the expansion of the soul; the growth of its pure beauty from muddy depths holds a benign spiritual promise."

An island or a boat floating on the sea is often used as a symbol of paradise, not only in dreams but also in poetry. For example, Shelley writes in "Epipsychidion":

> "An isle under Ionian skies,
> Beautiful as a wreck of Paradise."

This symbolism appears, too, in the same poet's "Lines Written Among the Euganean Hills", where we read:

> "Other flowering isles must be
> In the sea of Life and Agony ...
> We may live so happy there, ...
> ... our healing Paradise ..."

The unconscious itself may be symbolized in dreams by means of underground places.

A special word must be said about water, which symbolizes birth. All land mammals, from which the human race has sprung, are descended from creatures inhabiting the water. The stork that brings babies, according to the nursery legend, is said to get them out of a pond or well. In the myths of the births of heroes, the earliest of which is that of King Sargon of Akkad (*c.* 2800 B.C.), exposure in water and rescue from it play a major part. For example, the legend of Moses tells how he was found by Pharaoh's daughter in a basket floating in the water. (Exodus 2, 1-10.) Water also plays an essential part in the rite of baptism, which is a symbolic rebirth. Dr Ernest Jones points out that in hieroglyphic writing the sign for the female principle in the word for "woman" was a bowl of water. The spiritual rebirth implied in the decision to start a new form of life may be symbolized by the act of crossing water.

Other sexual symbols among natural objects are forests, grass, foliage, bushes, mushrooms and moss. The lily symbolizes innocence. Stones, according to Dr Erich Fromm, are symbols of sterility (cp. Matthew 7, 9).

When animals appear in dreams, as in fairy-tales, they, too, have a symbolic value. For example, children may be represented by small animals; in fact, the terms of endearment that are applied to children in waking life are frequently the names of animals, *e.g.*, chicken, duck, lamb. Children are also given the same name as the young of goats, *i.e.*, kids.

Fish, snails, cats, mice, snakes, frogs, lizards, reptiles, mussels and vermin all have a sexual significance. The pig is a symbol of fruitfulness.

The employment of the symbolism of snakes with a non-sexual significance may be observed in the following dream reported by a woman of forty-eight, who complained of having been very worried for many months about a matter touching the breaking of her association with a male friend.

She dreamed: "I was in our garden at home absolutely surrounded by brown snakes."

Asked for her associations to "snakes", she gave the following: "I have had a lot of trouble and worry. There has been a lot of talking behind my back about my friend and myself by so-called friends."

These associations show that the snakes symbolize: (1) the dreamer's troubles and worries (compare the expression, "to cherish a snake in one's bosom"—to meet with ingratitude or receive evil for good); and (2) her so-called friends who talk behind her back ("snakes in the grass").

An individual's parents may figure in his dreams in the shape of animals. The father may be represented by a dog or a horse; wild animals also represent passionate impulses or the persons who experience them, including the dreamer himself and other people of whom he is afraid. Pursuing beasts signify the dreamer's hostile tendencies, from which he is trying to escape. The mother may be represented by a spider or an octopus.

A pair of one kind, such as the dreamer's parents, may also be represented by a pair of another kind. The use of this symbolism may be observed in the following dream: "I went to look round the shops for a pair of shoes. I saw some grey suède shoes that took my fancy. On closer inspection, however, these proved to be only a pair of slippers, at the very much reduced price of one shilling."

The dreamer's associations showed that the pair of shoes represented a pair of marriage partners—her father and mother. The change that took place in the shoes during the dream corresponded to a wish and the reality that the wish sought to transcend. The dreamer wished that her parents were the ideal pair (the superior pair of shoes) that in reality they were not (the cheap slippers).

The marriage of the dreamer's parents, like the shoes, proved to be something other than the real thing. Her going shopping for a pair of shoes that took her fancy symbolized her childhood yearning for a father and mother who were a superior pair.

A Burmese symbol of the soul or psyche is a butterfly. In Greece, too, the goddess Psyche was usually represented with the wings of a butterfly. A certain psychology club has rather appropriately chosen a butterfly as a design on its letter heading accompanied by the words, "Know Yourself".

HUMAN BEINGS

Turning now to human beings, we find that exalted figures like kings and queens represent the dreamer's father and mother.

For example, a young radio operator dreamed that the late King George VI was touring a colony, in company with the then Mr Winston Churchill, and that while a broadcast was being made, he was asked to hold the microphone into which the King was speaking. The same man also dreamed that he had done something wrong and was taken before the Duke of Edinburgh, who readily forgave him.

The replacement of the real parents by these superior figures expresses the dreamer's yearning for the days of his childhood, when his father seemed to him the noblest and strongest of men and his mother the dearest and sweetest of women. We note incidentally that in ordinary speech a king is referred to as the father of his people. The use of this symbolism implies that the dreamer himself and his brothers and sisters may be represented by princes and princesses.

When dead persons appear as alive in our dreams, this signifies that we wish that they were alive. On the other hand, when persons still living appear as dead, we must assume that we wish that they were dead. Death itself is symbolized by a figure on a white horse; we read in The Revelation: "And I looked, and behold a pale horse: and his name that sat on him was Death." (Revelation 6, 8.)

A person whom one fails to recognize in a dream is actually the dreamer himself, while the mother may appear in a dream as a woman without a head. A number of strangers represents a secret, which is something known to only one or two persons. Here we see the principle of association by contrast at work again.

Not only individual persons but also parts of the human body may act as dream-symbols. Such symbols have chiefly a sexual value. Examples are the hand, foot, nose, eyes, teeth, tongue and bones. These are male symbols. According to a Mexican saga, a dead man's bone produced the father and mother of the present race of mankind. Female symbols are the ear, lips and mouth.

To illustrate, we may refer to the frequently recurring dreams in which teeth fall out or are extracted. These occur in both men and women and have a sexual value in either case. For example, a single 26-year-old Civil Servant had a constantly recurring dream in which his teeth became loose and fell out. A single 29-year-old farm worker dreamed of swallowing two teeth, and after that he felt a pain in the stomach.

We may also refer to actions performed by human beings. Some examples of this kind with their meanings are set forth below:

Symbol	Meaning
Departure on a journey	Death
Falling	Yielding to temptation
Entering or emerging from water	Birth
Flying, hovering or swimming	Repetition of childhood games involving movement
Climbing or descending stairs or ladders.	Mating

| Missing a train | Reassurance against fear of death |
| Walking through a suite of rooms | Marriage. |

Finally, the meaning of some abstract and miscellaneous ideas deserves mention. The presence of a number of things which are all the same indicates that some action is repeated a number of times. The concepts of right and left bear a moral significance as right and wrong. If the dreamer declares that he does not know the persons who appear in his dreams, this means that he knows them very well, but for some reason does not wish to recognize them.

If he comments especially on the vividness of a dream, it means that something in the latent dream-thoughts has really happened. For example, a married 34-year-old draughtsman said of a dream which he had while under gas in the dentist's chair: "This was so vivid that on coming round I could not believe it for some time." The dream corresponded to an experience which he had had twelve years previously.

A reference to the time of day in a dream indicates that the dream harks back to childhood. So, too, does a scene in which people look very small and far away, as though one were seeing them through the wrong end of a pair of opera-glasses. The idea of remoteness in time is indicated by remoteness in space.

Sometimes we find that one thing turns into something else in our dreams. This is the way that the dream-mind declares: "These two things are related as cause and effect." When two objects appear together in a dream, a choice between them may be implied. When we experience the sensation of being unable to move, the dream-mind is telling us that we are torn between conflicting impulses. The presence of the elements of contradiction, ridicule and derision is indicated by the introduction of some obvious absurdity into our dreams.

When games, dramatic performances and statements by drunken, insane or lying persons figure in dreams, they act as a denial of unpleasant truths. For example, a man dreamed: "One of my colleagues and I were play-acting. She was to steal something and I was to stop the burglar alarm from ringing." To depict the action of the dream as the performance of a play serves to deny the serious intent of the wish that the dream embodies. The burglar alarm probably represents the dreamer's conscience, which has to be silenced lest it criticize the theft intended in the dream.

CHAPTER XV

When Children Dream

THE dreams of children are noticeably free from the distortion which often makes it difficult for us to understand the dreams of adults. This does not mean that the dreams of children are invariably easier to interpret, but generally speaking they are briefer and clearer.

In many cases they relate to wishes which are much more readily accessible to the conscious mind, whereas the wishes that appear in the dreams of adults may be deeply repressed or hidden from consciousness.

It has been claimed that when a child recounts a dream to us, there is no need for us to obtain from the child any thoughts and memories of which the dream reminds him. On the other hand, if the child is willing to offer us such information, it would be foolish to ignore the additional light which it may throw on the dream.

A little girl of five had the following dream: "A big pancake with sharp teeth wanted to bite me." Asked if she was fond of pancakes, the little girl admitted that she was. Here the thought, "I would like to eat a big pancake," has contrived to appear in the dream with a minimum of distortion.

In order to avoid the accusation of greediness, the dreamer projects the wish into the pancake. "I would like to bite a pancake" becomes "A pancake would like to bite me." Besides gratifying the original wish in a slightly disguised form, the dream also holds a threat of punishment that enables the dreamer to atone for the feelings of guilt inspired by her greediness.

"IF I COULD FLY..."

A woman recalled the following dream, which she had when she was a small girl: "I was flying in at the window of a tall tenement building. A family of little Negro children leapt up with cries of joy and ran towards me the moment they caught sight of me. When I left them, they were seated round a roaring fire, talking and laughing happily, with the sunlight pouring through the window and lighting a comfortably furnished room."

The dreamer's associations were: "My only idea about little Negro children was that they lived in a warm sunny land surrounded by palm-trees, and enjoyed themselves consuming pineapples and bananas all day long."

When she was a child, the dreamer's family was very poor. The dream may, therefore, be interpreted as saying: "I wish my home were like this one. I wish I enjoyed myself in a warm sunny land, as do the Negro children. If I could fly, I would go there ..."

This dream of childhood was still remembered clearly a quarter of a century later, and will probably be remembered for the rest of the dreamer's life.

The wishes that appear in the dreams of adults are mostly "hangovers", as it were, from the dreamer's childhood. Freud goes right to the heart of the matter when he says: "We find the child and the child's impulses still living on in the dream." It is in the dreams of children, therefore, that we see these wishes in their pure form before they have become adulterated with the sophistications of adult life.

A transition stage between the simplicity of childhood and the more mature mentality of the adult is reflected in the dream of a 13-year-old boy: "I dreamed that I was coming home from school. On my way home I came to a 'Games School', where some of the boys were playing football. When they stopped I had a game. I was taught how to throw in."

His father told me that the lad had a keen sense of justice. He was quick to appreciate fairness and smarted under an injustice, whether it was done to himself or to anyone else. This dream of a football match confirms the father's words about his son's interest in "playing the game".

"Skating on Thin Ice"

A 4-year-old girl dreams of fairies skating.

The manifest content of this dream was derived from an event of the day before, when her mother told her a story about the rain fairies sliding down the window pane. The dream may deal with a wish to skate, since the child had expressed a desire for a pair of roller skates. Skating may also mean doing something forbidden, as we note from the saying, "skating on thin ice".

About a month later the same child dreamed of having a bath at Sunday school.

An infantile exhibitionist wish is at work here, manifesting itself under circumstances in which one would least expect it, thus emphasizing its tendency to attract attention to the nude body. The manifest content was, like that of the previous dream, clearly derived from events of the day before, since the dream occurred on a Saturday night after she had had a bath.

A young man recounted the following dream, which he had when he was about six or seven years old and which he described as "the first dream I can remember":

"I saw in detail a ring-net fishing-boat as clear as day, and there was a man in the picture."

His associations were: "At that time I was very interested in making boats and aeroplanes and taking mechanical toys to bits to see how they worked. One day I was trying to make a model of a ring-net fishing-boat. Why the man was there I don't know."

A Man Like Father

At a superficial level the dream presents a direct fulfilment of the wish to make the fishing-boat. Little boys like to make boats and aeroplanes, because this activity enables them to gratify in fantasy the wish to be a man like father. A boat or an aeroplane is what is known as a phallic symbol, *i.e.*, it represents the male organ. The man who appears in the dream is, therefore, the dreamer himself writ large. The dream also gratifies the dreamer's wish to be a grown-up man like the father-figure of the dream.

The fondness for taking mechanical toys to bits, which is by no means confined to small boys, will be seen to link up with the dream if we interpret it as a sublimation of sexual curiosity. The burning problem for the child is the question of how he himself is made; the interest in the working of toys and gadgets absorbs his curiosity about his own origin.

All the above dreams resemble the dreams of adults in that they are wish-fulfilments. The wishes that they fulfil are to some extent disguised, although the dreams of adults disguise their wishes to a much greater degree. As an illustration of a clear and unambiguous wish-fulfilment without the slightest degree of distortion, we may quote the following dream of a 6-year-old girl which epitomizes the matter in its simplest terms.

About three weeks before Christmas this youngster dreamed: "Father Christmas took me for a ride on his sleigh." Asked if she would like to go for a ride on his sleigh, she replied: "Yes". In the dream we have the direct, undisguised fulfilment of this wish.

"We see that these childhood dreams are not meaningless," writes Freud; "they are complete, comprehensible mental acts." Elsewhere he adds: "The common element in all these children's dreams is obvious. ... Even when the content of children's dreams becomes complicated and subtle, there is never any difficulty in recognizing them as wish-fulfilments."

CHAPTER XVI

Inspiration in Dreams

HAS it been known for creative inspiration and the solutions of problems to be found in dreams ?

Coleridge composed his poem, "Kubla Khan", in a dream, and was interrupted in writing it down by a call from a person on business.

William Archer, the playwright, obtained the plot of his famous thriller, *The Green Goddess*, from a dream.

Robert Louis Stevenson said that most of his plots came to him in dreams, including the idea of Jekyll and Hyde.

Professor Hilprecht, puzzled by the difficulty of two Babylonian inscriptions, was given the key to their meaning by an ancient Babylonian priest, who appeared to him in a dream.

David Parkinson, of the Bell Telephone Laboratory, dreamed that he was firing an electrically controlled anti-aircraft gun. On waking, he sketched the device, which was used by the United States Army.

A scientist who had completely failed to determine certain atomic linkages dreamed he was watching a dance. The pattern of changing partners gave the solution of his difficulty.

Plato in his *Phaedo* tells us that Socrates had a recurring dream in which he was commanded to "make and cultivate music". Socrates, says Plato, took it as an exhortation to study philosophy, which he had always regarded as "the noblest and best of music".

"The dream was bidding me to do," we read, "what I was already doing, in the same way that the competitor in a race is bidden by the spectators to run when he is already running. But I was not certain of this; for the dream might have meant music in the popular sense of the word, and being under sentence of death, and the festival giving me a respite, I thought that it would be safer for me to satisfy the scruple, and, in obedience to the dream, to compose a few verses before I departed."

The poetic muse to whose demands the dream gave expression

resulted in the composition of a hymn in honour of Apollo and a poetic version of the fables of Aesop.

The search for creative imagination is reflected in the dream of a single 22-year-old teacher who aspired to be an artist. He dreamed that he felt as if he could imagine wonderful scenery and landscapes.

"This means something to me," he commented, "because I have a strong desire to be able to paint as great artists do." He was forced to admit, however, that his mind was "so dull and unproductive."

This dream presents his desire as fulfilled, since to be a great painter he would need a strong imagination allied to a keen and productive mind. In other words, in his dream he seeks to compensate himself for the dullness and unproductiveness of mind that he experiences in his waking life.

How such a dream may lead to actual productiveness in waking life is illustrated by a report from a married 54-year-old Civil Servant with literary inclinations. "My recollections of my dreams are often enough distinct," he stated, "—sometimes so clear that they have been the subject of a completely written story."

This dreamer admits, however, that the dream imagination may not be wholly responsible for the finished product. "Perhaps the conscious imagination," he adds, "has contributed to its written completion."

THE STORY OF CAEDMON

One of the earliest examples of a dream of this type recorded in English literature is that of Caedmon, told by Bede (673-735) in his *Historia Ecclesiastica*. This famous work was translated into English at the end of the ninth century by scholars who worked under the direction of King Alfred.

Caedmon was a cowherd who, Bede tells us, "had lived a secular life up to the time that he was getting on in years and had never learned a song. Now often at the feast it was decreed for the sake of rejoicing that each in turn should sing to the harp.

"When he saw the harp coming near him, he arose in shame from the feast and went home. On one occasion he did this and left the house of the feast and had gone out to the cattle-shed, of which he had been put in charge that night. When he had duly laid his limbs to rest there and fallen asleep, someone stood before him in a dream and hailed him and called him by his name: 'Caedmon, sing me something'. Then he answered and said: 'I cannot sing; and so I left the feast and came hither, because I could not sing'. He who had spoken to him again said: 'However that may be, thou canst sing to me'. Then he said: 'What shall I sing?' He replied: 'Sing me the beginning of creation'.

"When he received that answer, he at once began to sing in praise of God the Creator verses and words which he had never heard before."

We are told that after he awakened Caedmon clearly remembered all that he had dreamed. He became a monk at Whitby Abbey, where he spent the rest of his life. He achieved great distinction with his newly-discovered gift of song, and was held in great repute by his brother-monks, none of whom was able to equal his poetic genius. He devoted his remaining years to composing poems of religion and piety, none of which unfortunately has survived. We learn, however, that their power was such as to inspire many to follow his example and take monastic vows, as well as to initiate a tradition of Anglo-Saxon religious poetry, which was, however, put an end to by the Danish invasions.

The interpretation of his dream is that Caedmon wished to overcome the sense of inferiority which he felt at not being able to improvise songs at the banqueting table. He sought to overcome this handicap directly by developing the ability which he lacked, rather than to compensate himself for it indirectly by cultivating some other ability that he already possessed. The dream that he had after retiring to the cowshed gratified his wish by drawing upon the fount of inspiration in his unconscious mind.

The literary creativeness of which we are capable in our dreams is further illustrated by the following report: "For many years I have repeatedly dreamed of writing works of great artistry. In my dreams words flow from my lips in dictation—sentences of such construction that on awakening I lie astonished, thinking of the beauty and merit of these literary outpourings. It seems as if the work of a great writer has photographed itself on my memory, and I am enabled to get a sort of screen replay of such a work. The word-play is such that I cannot consciously use so brilliantly."

This man, too, had a waking aspiration to be a writer. "Am I right in concluding," he asked, "that these literary outpourings are the result of this yearning finding an outlet ?"

Dreams may also present the solutions of difficult intellectual puzzles. Problems in chess or mathematics have been solved in this way. The dreamer goes to sleep after working hard at a problem and awakes with the solution in his mind. The process by which problems are solved both in dreams and in the waking state is called intuition.

Intuition is a form of thinking without the use of words. It contrasts with ordinary conscious thinking, which connects the "notions of things" with words. While words give precision to our thoughts, they may obscure new connections which intuition is useful in discovering.

One of the best examples is Kekule's discovery of the carbon ring during his sleep. He was dozing off while working at a study of organic compounds, and in his dream atoms at first chaotically tumbled before his eyes, then took shape and moved like a snake. Finally the snake, consisting of groups of atoms, bit its own tail. Kekule awoke with the discovery of the carbon ring.

CHAPTER XVII

Some Further Examples of Dream-Analysis

IN the first of the dreams that follow we see how one person may stand for another, while in the second we note an interesting use of a biblical quotation. The wish-fulfilment in both these dreams is clearly apparent. The possibility of one person standing for another also emerges from the analysis of the third dream, as, too, does the possibility of one action standing for another. This way in which the unconscious mind works is called "substitution".

The dream of sitting in a theatre reminds us of Shakespeare's lines from *As You Like It*:

"All the world's a stage,
And all the men and women merely players."

This is a further illustration of a point to which we have already alluded: that there is a common element of symbolism in both literature and dreams.

This dream, like the one that follows it, deals with childhood. The idea of exchanging one person for another also appears in the latter. Events of childhood, too, are the concern of the dream of riding in a car.

We may be able to get light on the meaning of a dream from the study of an analogous situation in mythology, as, for instance, in the next dream of "Achilles' heel". This is a particular example of the close connection in general that exists between psychology and mythology.[1]

Conflict in the mind between two desires is seen in the dream with which this chapter concludes.

Dream of Class-mate's Marriage

A single 35-year-old teacher dreamed that a school class-mate, who had died from an illness five years before, came to tell her she was getting married. At the time of the dream the dreamer's eldest sister was ill in hospital.

[1] See, for instance, the author's article, "Mind and Myth," *Psychology*, Vol. X, No. 7, November 1946.

Since the dreamer associated her sister's illness with the dream, we may assume that the class-mate represents her sister. If she tells the dreamer that she is getting married, it must mean that she has recovered from her illness. Therefore, we may take it that the dream presents the dreamer's wish that her sister would get well.

Dream of Reading the Bible

A Nigerian teacher dreamed that somebody gave him a Bible, in which he read: "And immediately he rose up before them, and took up that whereon he lay, and departed to his own house, glorifying God." (Luke 5, 25.) "I am always aiming very high", he said, "but I find it very hard and I become despondent. When I apply for something I am sure that I shall get the thing but in most cases I fail."

His aspirations receive expression in the dream through the recall of a verse which he has read in the past. This verse has stuck in his memory because it has reminded him that, like the man sick of the palsy, he, too, desires to rise. By gratifying his wish in this way the dream attempts to compensate him for his despondency and failure.

Dream of a Kiss in Employer's Presence

A woman desired a reconciliation with a man-friend who had broken off their association. She dreamed that the man and herself, who both worked for the same firm, were having a business discussion with their employer. Her friend got up, asked their employer to excuse him and kissed the dreamer.

"This sounds stupid because it is something we would never do," the woman declared. "We both knew that our employer agreed to our friendship and was pleased about it. So perhaps it is a wish on my part that he would kiss me, but not, of course, in front of my employer."

The key to the meaning of the dream is to be found in the dreamer's admission, "Perhaps it is a wish on my part that he would kiss me." We must agree with this part of her interpretation, although it leaves an important point unexplained. The dreamer denies that she would want to be kissed in front of her employer. And yet this is exactly what occurs in the dream.

There are two possible answers to this problem. (1) In the dream the employer does not represent himself, but someone else before whom the woman would not mind being kissed by her friend. (2) Kissing stands for something else that she would not object to her employer witnessing. Since he approved of the friendship between the two persons, we may assume that the dreamer would not mind his observing a reconciliation. This is, in fact, what she really wants and what the kiss may symbolize. (Compare the expressions, "kiss and be friends", "kiss and make up.")

Dream of Sitting in a Theatre

A widow of fifty-eight dreamed:

"I am sitting in the gallery of a theatre. In front there is a great expanse of very bright light. The place is stuffy and oppressive. There are people all round me, but I cannot distinguish any faces. Then someone takes me by the hand and leads me down some stairs."

Analysis of the dream yielded the following associations:

I am sitting in the gallery of a theatre: "I am too introspective."

The place is stuffy and oppressive: "I had a not too happy Victorian upbringing."

There are people all round me, but I cannot distinguish any faces: "I keep away from human contacts. I have a distaste for mixing with people."

Someone takes me by the hand and leads me down some stairs: "In my childhood there was very little affection."

The dream depicts the dreamer as a spectator looking back over her childhood, which, like the theatre, was stuffy and oppressive. The freedom and light that she missed as a child, on account of her Victorian upbringing, are represented by the expanse of very bright light. The dreamer's aversion to the society of other people is reflected in her inability to distinguish the faces round her in the dream. The thought, "I do not wish to know them," appears in the form, "I cannot tell who they are." The need of affection and someone to lean on is shown by the dreamer being taken by the hand and led like a child.

Some Further Examples of Dream-Analysis

Dream of Mother's Return

A single 26-year-old clerk reported the following dream:

"My mother came back to us again. It was as if she wanted to demonstrate her power, for she suddenly disappeared within my younger brother, who started speaking in my mother's tone of voice. The scene then changed to an airport building, through which a lot of people were passing. Their faces were stone grey, and it seemed to me as though they had come from another world."

The dreamer also reported the following associations:

"My mother died three years ago. In this dream she appeared very much younger than when she died, and in it both of us were conscious of the fact that she was dead. She seemed to have arisen to be with us again. When she was alive I always showed deep affection for her."

This dream, like the previous one, harks back to the days of the dreamer's childhood and says, "I remember my mother best as she was then; I wish that she were back with us again." The loss of identity which the young man's brother undergoes expresses the thought: "I would like to have her back even if it meant losing my brother." The reminder that his mother has passed away is given by the presence of the people from another world. The airport, which is a place of transition for persons departing and arriving, probably symbolizes death.

Dream of Riding in a Car

A man dreamed that he was a passenger in a car with two colleagues. The date was about 1925. He was quite undisturbed. He recognized a boy walking on the pavement as a boy he knew in his school-days but older than he. He picked up a newspaper which bore the date 1923, and remarked that he was only five years old then. The town was very untidy.

In association with this dream the man disclosed that he was the youngest of three children. His mother died when he was four, and his father remarried a few months afterwards. "We children were boarded out," he said, "and during my school-days I lived at nine different addresses." His father became bankrupt, his wife left him and he committed suicide.

The date of the events of the dream and the discovery of the date of the newspaper show that the dream deals with the dreamer's childhood. This is confirmed by the actual reference occurring in the dream to his age at the time of publication of the newspaper. The boy walking on the pavement may, therefore, be taken as representing himself as a child, and the other two occupants of the car may be identified with his two sisters. The fact that the boy on the pavement does not represent the boy he knew at school is indicated by his being older than he was when the dreamer knew him.

The condition of the town symbolizes the dreamer's childhood, which was also untidy in a different sense. The dream is a wishfulfilment. It expresses the thought: "I wish things were not as they are," *i.e.*, "I wish I had had a childhood that was 'quite undisturbed'." In view of the nature of the events that disturbed his childhood years, the appearance of this wish in the dream is easy to understand.

Dream of "Achilles' Heel"

"My sister was bleeding from the ankle and this was incurable." This was a dream of a young single woman of twenty-nine. Her associations to the dream were that her sister represented herself, and that the dream depicted the dreamer's attitude towards herself, which was one of hopelessness.

The incurable bleeding ankle reminds us of Achilles, one of the leaders of the Greeks against Troy. His mother dipped him in the river Styx to render him invulnerable, but the heel by which she held him was not wetted, and he died of a wound in the heel from an arrow shot by the Trojan, Paris.

The dream meant that menstruation was the dreamer's "Achilles' heel" or weak spot. In her love life she had sought to deny the basic fact that she was a woman. The dreamer despaired of being cured of repeatedly falling in love with members of her own sex. In other words, the dream, by depicting something typically feminine, gives vent to the repressed femininity of the dreamer's nature.

Dream of Ambition versus Laziness

The eldest son of a poor family, who had failed in his Civil

Service examinations, dreamed: "I am driving a car or a motor bike and doing my utmost with the throttle or accelerator, but the vehicle just seems to go slower."

"My dreams of becoming someone are slowly diminishing," he stated. "I dearly want to better myself." Then he went on to recount an experience that happened to him a few weeks before he had the dream: "I partly awakened to realize that I could not move a single muscle for a second or two, until I had forced myself out of it with a quick movement."

The interpretation of the dream, in his own words, was: "I lack ability to concentrate in order to better myself. I have always been mentally lazy. To be able to study for a decent situation is my desire. I have not, however, decided on any particular profession."

Besides reflecting the two conflicting tendencies of ambition and laziness, the dream is also of interest on account of the half-waking experience connected with it. Another person, a 24-year-old shop assistant, stated:

"I go to sleep, then wake up later and find I can't move a muscle. Eventually I manage with great effort to move a little. From correspondence in a newspaper I find that I am probably suffering from 'sleep paralysis'. I also feel a falling or sinking sensation in the region of the diaphragm."

The condition which these two people describe is probably due to a form of self-hypnosis. They have accepted the suggestion that they cannot move a muscle, and this suggestion takes effect until they counter it with the suggestion that they can. The readiness of the sleeper's position in bed to lend itself to this self-induced immobility is due to his previous experience of lying immobile in a cramped space, *i.e.*, during pre-natal life.

Going to bed and falling asleep are in themselves actions which attempt to gratify the individual's unconscious wish to return to the comfort and security of life in the womb.

At the same time as the second person experiences the immobility of the muscles, a cessation of digestion probably occurs. That is to say, the muscle of the stomach is affected as well as the muscles of the limbs. This probably accounts for the falling or sinking sensation of which he complains.

CHAPTER XVIII

Typical Dreams

A DISCUSSION of dreams would be incomplete without some reference to certain dreams which are described as "typical". They are given this name because they occur with great frequency among a good many people.

A very well-known example is the typical dream of missing a train. This is considered to refer to a journey that everyone is compelled to make—the journey through life to the grave. A person who has died is spoken of as the "departed", as though he had set out on a journey. This dream reflects the dreamer's unconscious wish to reassure himself against the fear of death.

In some cases the emphasis is on the short time allowed to catch the train. For example, a 52-year-old housewife dreams: "I am packing feverishly at only very short notice to be ready to catch a train or ship." The idea of packing feverishly is probably a comment on the shortness of the span of life. When we want to make the most of our time, we say that we have to "pack in" as much as possible. Catching a train or ship symbolizes dying.

Another housewife, aged forty-six, describes the same dream in almost the same words: "I am trying to sort out and pack things for going on a journey, sometimes in a train and at other times on a ship. I am in a desperate hurry and very muddled."

GOING TO THE STATION

"I visit a railway station," reported another dreamer. "I do not see myself on the platform, yet I know that I am there. It is always the same station. This dream recurs *very* often."

The dream of going to the station is a variation of the typical dream of missing a train. Going to the station implies catching a train, which, as we have seen, symbolizes dying. Where a person goes to the station but does not catch the train, such a dream says in effect, "I shall not die". In other words, the dream is intended to reassure the dreamer against a fear of death.

In other cases the dreamer catches his train but never gets to his destination. The same meaning must probably be ascribed to such a dream as to a dream of missing the train.

CATCHING THE TRAIN

A 59-year-old housewife reports: "During the last three years I have noted that, instead of missing the train, ship, bus or plane, I now dream of catching it, and experience the actual sensation of travelling."

This person had been widowed very suddenly, being left with only a small capital and no pension. This compelled her to turn her thoughts to earning her own living by part-time work, "so that my mind can be free from financial worry or limitation". We may assume that the loss of her husband had brought home to her the reality of death and served to decrease her fear. Consequently, there was no need for her any longer to go on reassuring herself by dreaming of missing the train. The dream of catching the train might be interpreted as expressing the wish: "I would like to join my husband", *i.e.*, "I would like to take the same journey that he has taken."

A single 51-year-old lady dreamed: "I am waiting for a bus to take me to work. I always get on the bus but I never get to work." We might be inclined to suppose that the dream reflects her wish not to go to work. She admitted that she was not very fond of her present occupation. This interpretation, while probably true, lays itself open to the objection that it is too superficial. The fact that she never reaches her destination may mean the same as not catching the bus at all—it is her means of attempting to reassure herself against the fear of death.

While undertaking self-analysis for the purpose of relieving the after effects of a nervous breakdown that had occurred twelve months before, this person ceased to experience the dream that has just been described. This suggests that the work of self-analysis enabled her to confront the fear of death and dispose of it on a rational level, thus making it unnecessary for her to continue to reassure herself against it by means of her dream.

FLOATING ON AIR

The other set of typical dreams that deserves to be discussed is those concerned with flying, floating through the air, and falling.

"I dreamed of flying as if I had wings," declared Mr A. From a study of his background we learn that he was troubled with feelings of inferiority. He was seeking to compensate himself for them by means of a fantasy or day-dream of having a son who would be all that his father was not.

We attempt to put on the dream of flying an interpretation that brings it into close connection with the dreamer's problems as a whole. The act of soaring over the heads of other people provides another compensation for feelings of inferiority. It is as though the dreamer were saying: "Look at me! See how clever I am. I can fly! I'm far above everybody else!"

DREAMS OF FALLING

"What does it mean when one often dreams of falling?" asked a single 42-year-old lady cashier. A single 23-year-old market gardener put the same question. "I sometimes dream of falling from some high building, or over some steep precipice, and just when about to hit the ground, I waken. What is the explanation of this?"

The answer given by psycho-analysis is: "These dreams reproduce impressions of childhood; they relate, that is, to games involving movement, which are extraordinarily attractive to children. In after years they repeat these experiences in dreams; but in the dreams they leave out the hands which held them up, so that they float or fall unsupported."

A women's periodical published a feature which presented a discussion on dreams between a doctor and a woman patient. The patient, a Miss T., complains of recurring nightmares, from which she wakes up in a fright. In her dreams she finds herself walking a very narrow plank which stretches for miles over the sea. Sometimes she dreams of falling all the way down a mountain into the valley below. The patient then asks bluntly: "What causes these nightmares, Doctor?"

The doctor replies cautiously: "Sometimes the cause is entirely physical. Usually, though, it is emotional; but it may quite easily be both."

He then goes on to suggest that the dreams may be due to hunger, indigestion, a bad cold or difficulty in breathing. In his opinion the terror that the patient experiences is a reaction to the physical symptoms that accompany these conditions.

The patient then admits that she has catarrh, but points out that she had it before the nightmares started. The doctor says next that bad dreams may be caused by worry. This prompts the patient to acknowledge that some work that she had on her mind at the office may have caused the nightmares. The doctor agrees, although he insists that the catarrh must have had a hand in it as well.

The chief criticism that we must offer is that the handling of the problem is superficial. The doctor has neatly side-stepped the real problem by ignoring the subject-matter of the dreams. Had he examined this he might have discovered the wish which it conceals. He might then have seen that the dreams were not caused by worry, but that both the dreams and the worry were reactions to the wish. The patient had obviously disowned this wish, and in the absence of insight blamed the worry on her work.

If we examine the two forms that the nightmares took, we see at once that the common element in them is the idea of falling. When this idea occurs in a dream, it is to be interpreted in a figurative sense, *e.g.*, falling in love, a fall from grace, falling a victim to temptation.

The patient may have entertained some pleasurable thought of this kind. For some reason or other she may have put it away from her, so that she no longer remained aware of it. While one part of her mind was tempted to yield, another part disapproved of the idea. The two sides of this mental conflict are neatly expressed in the nightmares. In one of the dreams we see the wish to fall being gratified; in the other we note the patient's wish to keep to the straight and narrow.

CHAPTER XIX

Miscellaneous Questions on Dreams

Do animals dream?

We do not know for certain. We cannot question an animal on its experience, nor can it report its experience to us. Hence, whether we reply "Yes" or "No", our answer must be based on belief, not on knowledge. The writer's belief is that some animals may dream. The slight muscular movements that they make suggest that the cat or dog taking a nap on the hearth-rug may be dreaming. Even if dreams occur in animals, however, we can have no idea of what they dream about. The whole matter, indeed, cannot go beyond the stage of insecurely founded speculation, and whatever answer we base upon our personal belief deserves to be treated with caution. We must not conclude that an animal thinks and feels as we should in the same situation.

Are nightmares related to insomnia?

If a person who is harbouring some violently repressed desire learns from experience how frightening are the dreams which give expression to this desire, he sometimes prefers to stay awake rather than confront his repressed desire in sleep. This state of affairs is generally known as insomnia, although it would be more appropriately called hypnophobia. The victim is not so much unable to sleep as afraid to sleep.

I have read that what are known as the three "absolutes" are said to manifest themselves in a person's dreams. Can you tell me what they are?

They are the immortality of the soul, the striving for superiority and the omnipotence of thought. The individual cannot dream that he does not exist. If he dreams of his own death, he always survives as a spectator. Similarly, he is able to perform any feat he wants to, and he is able to gratify any wish by thinking of its fulfilment. These motifs often appear in fairy-tales, which like dreams reflect the childhood of the race embedded in the unconscious mind, which is the child-mind.

Can we train ourselves to remember our dreams better?

The power of conscious recall of dreams diminishes rapidly on waking, and a deliberate effort to recall a dream often accelerates the process of forgetting.

A single 37-year-old South African psychologist describes the successful method which he uses for remembering his dreams as follows: "My recollections of my dreams are distinct and connected after I apply a system of 'listening relaxation' as soon as I wake in the mornings." It is also possible to rely on a subsequent event evoking a train of association that leads to the recall of a forgotten dream. "I remember most of my dreams," declared a married 31-year-old stone-carver, "either upon awakening or some time after, when *some chance happening reveals the dream to my memory.*"

Why do some people claim they never dream?

"I cannot ever remember being conscious of having dreamed," reports a man from Cardiff. "Some people I know can give vivid accounts of their dreams, and, in fact, admit that they dream every night." Here are three possible explanations: (1) Such a person has a poor memory for his dreams. (2) His dreams are so heavily censored by his conscience that they never emerge into consciousness. (3) His faculty of making mental pictures, which are the stuff that gives form to his dreams, is not strongly developed.

Do blind people dream?

This question was put to a man blind from birth in an article, "The World I've Never Seen", published in *Psychology* Magazine for September, 1948. Here is the answer he gave: "I dream, but I cannot see. One imagines in terms of sound and touch, etc." In a case where a person has become blind since birth, mental pictures or visual imagery may or may not appear in his dreams.

If the psychological theory of dreams is true, why should I always have had bad dreams after I have eaten a heavy supper? Surely such dreams are due to indigestion?

One cannot deny that a heavy supper may cause you to have bad dreams. The dream-process is set working by the disturbed condition of your digestion. But there is another problem here apart from the fact that you dream. There is also the problem of *what* you dream, and this is determined by your unconscious wishes. No two persons who have a heavy meal last thing at night dream exactly alike, because their dreams are always a reflection of their buried desires.

For years I have experienced a certain type of mental picture which appears just on going to sleep or waking. These pictures can be faces or scenes, usually in colour. They are very vivid indeed. Can you tell me anything about these?

They are known as hypnagogic visions and occur in healthy individuals, especially if they are both mentally excited and physically exhausted. In them something that has been experienced in infancy and then forgotten re-emerges. Something that the child has seen while he could still hardly speak now forces its way into consciousness.

Do we dream all the time we are asleep or only part of the time?

"Whether dreams pervade all of the sleep period or only certain portions of it remains an unsolved problem. Systematic recording of dreams results in data strongly favouring the latter possibility. Calkins and Sanford many years ago made one of the few careful studies of this problem, and found that about three-quarters of their dreams occurred after four o'clock in the morning. Their method was to provide themselves with the necessary conveniences for recording, and then to retire with the intention of waking and recording the nature and time of such dreams as appeared. The results are in conformity with the course of the normal sleep curve, with the greatest number of dreams indicated when sleep is most shallow. Later Berrien, with a somewhat better method, found that the number of dreams fell off toward the third hour of the sleep period, after which it rose steadily. By the fifth and sixth hours the dream frequency was greater than for the first hour.

"It may well be argued that results obtained by any of the methods here used are inconclusive, since the subjects could obviously report only the dreams which disturbed sleep to the point of waking, or which could be recalled upon waking. Perhaps there were as many dreams in the other parts of the sleep period which the condition of the subjects prevented from being recorded or recalled. Some psychologists have even argued that sleep is never dreamless. No method has so far been devised whereby the problem can be satisfactorily attacked." (D. B. Klein: *Abnormal Psychology*, pp. 203-4.)

You have claimed that dreams are as old as the race. Can you give any more examples of dreams recorded in ancient times?

Between the outstretched paws of the Sphinx near the Pyramids of Gizeh a large slab of granite bears an inscription recording a dream of Thutmose IV of the XVIIIth Dynasty of Egyptian kings (*c.* 1573 B.C.).

According to the inscription, Thutmose, before he ascended the throne, was out hunting one day, when he decided to rest at noon and fell asleep in the shadow of the Sphinx. He dreamed that the Sphinx, which was regarded as an embodiment of the sun-god Harmachis, promised him the double crown of Upper and Lower Egypt if he would clear away the sand which had nearly engulfed its body.

Although the latter part of the inscription is too badly weathered to be legible, it may be surmised that it related how the wish which revealed itself in the prince's dream came true when he later succeeded to the crown.

The Roman orator Cicero in the first part of his essay *On Divination* quotes many instances of dreams from literature, history and legend, all of which came true. In the second part he attacks the idea of divination, which he stigmatizes as nonsense. He professes contempt for predictive dreams, including one of his own which came true.

He is said, however, to have had another dream which so impressed him that he took it seriously. In this dream Cicero saw a young man who was singled out by Jupiter to attain supreme power in Rome. Next day Cicero saw a young man whom he instantly recognised as the hero of his dream. He was Julius Caesar's nephew, Octavius, who subsequently became the Emperor Augustus.

Afterwards the orator cultivated the young man, and the relations between the two became most cordial. This did not, however, prevent Cicero and his brother Quintus from later being assassinated. In his essay *On Dreams* Sir Thomas Browne remarks drily: "Cicero is much to be pitied, who, having excellently discoursed on the vanity of dreams, was yet undone by the flatterie of his owne."

You have referred only to the dreams of sleep. What can you tell us about day-dreams?

Day-dreams, too, are imaginary gratifications of wishes. The day-dream differs from the night-dream in being more free from control and criticism. Although both are imaginary wish-fulfilments, compensating the individual for what is denied him in the world of reality, the day-dream is concerned with wishes which are less deeply repressed.

A young man recalled that as a boy of fourteen he had a day-dream of engaging in a death-struggle with a Japanese soldier. "The war in the far East was in progress at the time," he said, "and I used to spend hours at a time visualising myself in a death-grip with an opponent."

"At thirteen," he added, "I first wanted to be 'cock of the walk'. I looked forward to getting a job, but I wasn't allowed by my father to accept the one of my choice. I am allergic to my father. He makes me feel as if I am trying to repress a feeling that keeps coming up within me. I feel irritated when he is around. I experience a wave of emotion coming over me. He just makes me feel aggressive."

Not being allowed to follow the career of his choice would arouse hostility towards his father, who is represented by the Japanese soldier. His fantasy of engaging in a death-struggle provided an outlet for the aggressiveness that he admitted he experienced.

Day-dreaming is a state of consciousness in which the mind tries to achieve by fantasy the indulgence which it longs for in reality but has been unable to obtain. It is a relapse of consciousness into an infantile method of thinking. A certain amount of day-dreaming is harmless, but when over-indulged in, it indicates that the day-dreamer is frustrated in reality.

The difference between day-dreaming and the exercise of constructive imagination is that the former is an end in itself, whereas the latter is a means to the end of effective action. Day-dreaming is the result of an effort to escape the demands of life. Constructive imagination is an effort to reproduce in the world of reality those things and conditions which hold the mind enthralled during flights of fancy.

One type of day-dream is the fantasy of display, in which the day-dreamer, in circumstances at variance with real life, performs a feat which wins applause. For example, a single 24-year-old plumber states: "I often imagine myself carrying out some great feat of heroism, and having my name and photo in the local newspaper commending me for bravery."

Another is the fantasy of homage, in which the day-dreamer does a service to win approval. For example, a married 32-year-old decorator states: "My day-dreams are mainly based on power to do good, to make others happy by being in a position to help. They are always centred around happiness and the desire to make others happy in order to be looked up to and to be a favourite."

In both these cases the day-dreamer exalts himself in circumstances in which the inhibitions and restraints of his environment and his own shortcomings are ignored.

What is the meaning of the dream in which one is caught wearing few or no clothes in public?

"I am in a crowded place with people milling round me," stated a young woman, describing her recurrent dream, "and I suddenly realise I am inadequately clothed. I feel terrible shame and embarrassment, and yet cannot get out of the crowd. Two friends of mine also have this very same dream."

The dream of being naked or inadequately clothed may mean that the dreamer would like to expose to other people that aspect of her personality which she regards as her true self. The dream reflects a wish on the part of the dreamer to let others see her as she really is. The embarrassment in the dream may reflect a fear of the disapproval of others if the dreamer dares to be herself. A metaphorical exposure of this kind is symbolized by a literal one, as is also done in ordinary speech in such expressions as "the naked truth", "the naked heart".

CHAPTER XX

Conclusion

THERE are many topics connected with dreams that space will not permit one to touch upon, much as the reader would perhaps wish one to do so. For example, there are other typical dreams that might have been mentioned. Interesting dreams, worthy of discussion, can also be garnered from sources such as literary history. No attempt has been made to approach the problem of dream-interpretation from any point of view other than that of the psychology of the unconscious.

The author has excused himself from treating these topics on the ground of lack of space. To be honest, there is another reason. To shelter behind lack of space is really an excuse. My silence is due also to ignorance. To tell the truth, I am glad not to have to treat some of these subjects, as I know very little about them. This is a shortcoming which in time will, I hope, be made good by those to whom I am indebted for accounts of their dreams. To all who have so liberally allowed me access to their mental life, and to the authorities whom I have quoted, I am deeply grateful.

I would like to pass on a suggestion to the reader of this book. Anyone who is seriously interested in this subject should not fail to read the work from which I have also drawn heavily. Writing thirty-one years after the first appearance of his *The Interpretation of Dreams*, Professor Sigmund Freud declared: "It contains, even according to my present-day judgment, the most valuable of all the discoveries it has been my good fortune to make."

One must agree with the author's admission that the book cannot be described as easy to read. Yet anyone who takes the trouble to go through it will be amply rewarded. He will be able to echo Freud's now opinion that "Insight such as this falls to one's lot but once in a lifetime."

Before this book was written, no one had said anything that threw any real light on dreams. One might go further and add that no one has said anything since that is worthy to rank with the profound insight of this masterpiece.

Even psychologists who do not share the psycho-analytical viewpoint acknowledge the value of this work. For example, Lewis Way, in *Adler's Place in Psychology*, writes: "Anyone who has absorbed its contents can fairly be said to have understood the attitude to life and the main forms of thought which make up the world of psycho-analysis."

The psycho-analytical theory of dreams is often attacked on the ground that it deals too much with "sex". Many critics attribute to the psychology of the unconscious the teaching that all dreams are based on repressed sexual wishes. This idea must be specifically refuted. The claim that all dreams call for a sexual interpretation is quite foreign to *The Interpretation of Dreams*. In his autobiography the founder of psycho-analysis says: "I have never maintained the assertion which has so often been ascribed to me that dream-interpretation shows that all dreams have a sexual content or are derived from sexual motive forces." Sufficient non-sexual dreams have been described in the present volume to support this contention.

The fact remains, however, that "dreams which are conspicuously innocent commonly embody crude erotic wishes". This should cause us no surprise when we reflect that in our civilization the sexual impulse is the one that regularly undergoes the most repression.

What is the value of dream-interpretation? Let the late Dr A. A. Brill answer this question. "He who is well versed in the technique of interpreting dreams," he says, "possesses the key to neurotic and psychotic symptoms, to myths, fairy tales, folklore, and religious rites." Or in the words of Freud himself: "The interpretation of dreams is the royal road to a knowledge of the unconscious activities of the mind." The importance of knowing this element may be judged from its designation as "the general basis of psychical life".

"The unconscious," we read, "is the true psychical reality."

"I would look for the theoretical value of the study of dreams," continues the author, "in the contributions it makes to psychological knowledge".

INDEX

Index

A Personal Word From Melvin Powers
Publisher, Wilshire Book Company

Dear Friend:

My goal is to publish interesting, informative, and inspirational books. You can help me accomplish this by answering the following questions, either by phone or by mail. Or, if convenient for you, I would welcome the opportunity to visit with you in my office and hear your comments in person.

Did you enjoy reading this book? Why?

Would you enjoy reading another similar book?

What idea in the book impressed you the most?

If applicable to your situation, have you incorporated this idea in your daily life?

Is there a chapter that could serve as a theme for an entire book? Please explain.

If you have an idea for a book, I would welcome discussing it with you. If you already have one in progress, write or call me concerning possible publication. I can be reached at (213) 875-1711 or (213) 983-1105.

Sincerely yours,

Melvin Powers

12015 Sherman Road
North Hollywood, California 91605

MELVIN POWERS SELF-IMPROVEMENT LIBRARY

ASTROLOGY
_____ASTROLOGY: HOW TO CHART YOUR HOROSCOPE *Max Heindel*   3.00
_____ASTROLOGY: YOUR PERSONAL SUN-SIGN GUIDE *Beatrice Ryder*   3.00
_____ASTROLOGY FOR EVERYDAY LIVING *Janet Harris*   2.00
_____ASTROLOGY MADE EASY *Astarte*   3.00
_____ASTROLOGY MADE PRACTICAL *Alexandra Kayhle*   3.00
_____ASTROLOGY, ROMANCE, YOU AND THE STARS *Anthony Norvell*   4.00
_____MY WORLD OF ASTROLOGY *Sydney Omarr*   5.00
_____THOUGHT DIAL *Sydney Omarr*   3.00
_____WHAT THE STARS REVEAL ABOUT THE MEN IN YOUR LIFE *Thelma White*   3.00

BRIDGE
_____BRIDGE BIDDING MADE EASY *Edwin B. Kantar*   5.00
_____BRIDGE CONVENTIONS *Edwin B. Kantar*   5.00
_____BRIDGE HUMOR *Edwin B. Kantar*   3.00
_____COMPETITIVE BIDDING IN MODERN BRIDGE *Edgar Kaplan*   4.00
_____DEFENSIVE BRIDGE PLAY COMPLETE *Edwin B. Kantar*   10.00
_____HOW TO IMPROVE YOUR BRIDGE *Alfred Sheinwold*   2.00
_____IMPROVING YOUR BIDDING SKILLS *Edwin B. Kantar*   4.00
_____INTRODUCTION TO DEFENDER'S PLAY *Edwin B. Kantar*   3.00
_____SHORT CUT TO WINNING BRIDGE *Alfred Sheinwold*   3.00
_____TEST YOUR BRIDGE PLAY *Edwin B. Kantar*   3.00
_____WINNING DECLARER PLAY *Dorothy Hayden Truscott*   4.00

BUSINESS, STUDY & REFERENCE
_____CONVERSATION MADE EASY *Elliot Russell*   2.00
_____EXAM SECRET *Dennis B. Jackson*   2.00
_____FIX-IT BOOK *Arthur Symons*   2.00
_____HOW TO DEVELOP A BETTER SPEAKING VOICE *M. Hellier*   2.00
_____HOW TO MAKE A FORTUNE IN REAL ESTATE *Albert Winnikoff*   4.00
_____INCREASE YOUR LEARNING POWER *Geoffrey A. Dudley*   2.00
_____MAGIC QF NUMBERS *Robert Tocquet*   2.00
_____PRACTICAL GUIDE TO BETTER CONCENTRATION *Melvin Powers*   2.00
_____PRACTICAL GUIDE TO PUBLIC SPEAKING *Maurice Forley*   3.00
_____7 DAYS TO FASTER READING *William S. Schaill*   3.00
_____SONGWRITERS RHYMING DICTIONARY *Jane Shaw Whitfield*   5.00
_____SPELLING MADE EASY *Lester D. Basch & Dr. Milton Finkelstein*   2.00
_____STUDENT'S GUIDE TO BETTER GRADES *J. A. Rickard*   3.00
_____TEST YOURSELF—Find Your Hidden Talent *Jack Shafer*   2.00
_____YOUR WILL & WHAT TO DO ABOUT IT *Attorney Samuel G. Kling*   3.00

CALLIGRAPHY
_____ADVANCED CALLIGRAPHY *Katherine Jeffares*   6.00
_____CALLIGRAPHY—The Art of Beautiful Writing *Katherine Jeffares*   5.00

CHESS & CHECKERS
_____BEGINNER'S GUIDE TO WINNING CHESS *Fred Reinfeld*   3.00
_____BETTER CHESS—How to Play *Fred Reinfeld*   2.00
_____CHECKERS MADE EASY *Tom Wiswell*   2.00
_____CHESS IN TEN EASY LESSONS *Larry Evans*   3.00
_____CHESS MADE EASY *Milton L. Hanauer*   3.00
_____CHESS MASTERY—A New Approach *Fred Reinfeld*   2.00
_____CHESS PROBLEMS FOR BEGINNERS *edited by Fred Reinfeld*   2.00
_____CHESS SECRETS REVEALED *Fred Reinfeld*   2.00
_____CHESS STRATEGY—An Expert's Guide *Fred Reinfeld*   2.00
_____CHESS TACTICS FOR BEGINNERS *edited by Fred Reinfeld*   3.00
_____CHESS THEORY & PRACTICE *Morry & Mitchell*   2.00
_____HOW TO WIN AT CHECKERS *Fred Reinfeld*   2.00
_____1001 BRILLIANT WAYS TO CHECKMATE *Fred Reinfeld*   3.00
_____1001 WINNING CHESS SACRIFICES & COMBINATIONS *Fred Reinfeld*   3.00
_____SOVIET CHESS *Edited by R. G. Wade*   3.00

COOKERY & HERBS
_____CULPEPER'S HERBAL REMEDIES *Dr. Nicholas Culpeper*   2.00

____FAST GOURMET COOKBOOK *Poppy Cannon*	2.50
____GINSENG The Myth & The Truth *Joseph P. Hou*	3.00
____HEALING POWER OF HERBS *May Bethel*	3.00
____HEALING POWER OF NATURAL FOODS *May Bethel*	3.00
____HERB HANDBOOK *Dawn MacLeod*	3.00
____HERBS FOR COOKING AND HEALING *Dr. Donald Law*	2.00
____HERBS FOR HEALTH—How to Grow & Use Them *Louise Evans Doole*	3.00
____HOME GARDEN COOKBOOK—Delicious Natural Food Recipes *Ken Kraft*	3.00
____MEDICAL HERBALIST *edited by Dr. J. R. Yemm*	3.00
____NATURAL FOOD COOKBOOK *Dr. Harry C. Bond*	3.00
____NATURE'S MEDICINES *Richard Lucas*	3.00
____VEGETABLE GARDENING FOR BEGINNERS *Hugh Wiberg*	2.00
____VEGETABLES FOR TODAY'S GARDENS *R. Milton Carleton*	2.00
____VEGETARIAN COOKERY *Janet Walker*	3.00
____VEGETARIAN COOKING MADE EASY & DELECTABLE *Veronica Vezza*	3.00
____VEGETARIAN DELIGHTS—A Happy Cookbook for Health *K. R. Mehta*	2.00
____VEGETARIAN GOURMET COOKBOOK *Joyce McKinnel*	3.00

GAMBLING & POKER

____ADVANCED POKER STRATEGY & WINNING PLAY *A. D. Livingston*	3.00
____HOW NOT TO LOSE AT POKER *Jeffrey Lloyd Castle*	3.00
____HOW TO WIN AT DICE GAMES *Skip Frey*	3.00
____HOW TO WIN AT POKER *Terence Reese & Anthony T. Watkins*	2.00
____SECRETS OF WINNING POKER *George S. Coffin*	3.00
____WINNING AT CRAPS *Dr. Lloyd T. Commins*	3.00
____WINNING AT GIN *Chester Wander & Cy Rice*	3.00
____WINNING AT POKER—An Expert's Guide *John Archer*	3.00
____WINNING AT 21—An Expert's Guide *John Archer*	3.00
____WINNING POKER SYSTEMS *Norman Zadeh*	3.00

HEALTH

____BEE POLLEN *Lynda Lyngheim & Jack Scagnetti*	3.00
____DR. LINDNER'S SPECIAL WEIGHT CONTROL METHOD *P. G. Lindner, M.D.*	1.50
____HELP YOURSELF TO BETTER SIGHT *Margaret Darst Corbett*	3.00
____HOW TO IMPROVE YOUR VISION *Dr. Robert A. Kraskin*	3.00
____HOW YOU CAN STOP SMOKING PERMANENTLY *Ernest Caldwell*	3.00
____MIND OVER PLATTER *Peter G. Lindner, M.D.*	3.00
____NATURE'S WAY TO NUTRITION & VIBRANT HEALTH *Robert J. Scrutton*	3.00
____NEW CARBOHYDRATE DIET COUNTER *Patti Lopez-Pereira*	1.50
____PSYCHEDELIC ECSTASY *William Marshall & Gilbert W. Taylor*	2.00
____QUICK & EASY EXERCISES FOR FACIAL BEAUTY *Judy Smith-deal*	2.00
____QUICK & EASY EXERCISES FOR FIGURE BEAUTY *Judy Smith-deal*	2.00
____REFLEXOLOGY *Dr. Maybelle Segal*	3.00
____YOU CAN LEARN TO RELAX *Dr. Samuel Gutwirth*	3.00
____YOUR ALLERGY—What To Do About It *Allan Knight, M.D.*	3.00

HOBBIES

____BEACHCOMBING FOR BEGINNERS *Norman Hickin*	2.00
____BLACKSTONE'S MODERN CARD TRICKS *Harry Blackstone*	3.00
____BLACKSTONE'S SECRETS OF MAGIC *Harry Blackstone*	2.00
____COIN COLLECTING FOR BEGINNERS *Burton Hobson & Fred Reinfeld*	2.00
____ENTERTAINING WITH ESP *Tony 'Doc' Shiels*	2.00
____400 FASCINATING MAGIC TRICKS YOU CAN DO *Howard Thurston*	3.00
____HOW I TURN JUNK INTO FUN AND PROFIT *Sari*	3.00
____HOW TO WRITE A HIT SONG & SELL IT *Tommy Boyce*	7.00
____JUGGLING MADE EASY *Rudolf Dittrich*	2.00
____MAGIC MADE EASY *Byron Wels*	2.00
____STAMP COLLECTING FOR BEGINNERS *Burton Hobson*	2.00
____STAMP COLLECTING FOR FUN & PROFIT *Frank Cetin*	2.00

HORSE PLAYERS' WINNING GUIDES

____BETTING HORSES TO WIN *Les Conklin*	3.00
____ELIMINATE THE LOSERS *Bob McKnight*	3.00
____HOW TO PICK WINNING HORSES *Bob McKnight*	3.00
____HOW TO WIN AT THE RACES *Sam (The Genius) Lewin*	3.00
____HOW YOU CAN BEAT THE RACES *Jack Kavanagh*	3.00
____MAKING MONEY AT THE RACES *David Barr*	3.00

_____PAYDAY AT THE RACES *Les Conklin*	3.00
_____SMART HANDICAPPING MADE EASY *William Bauman*	3.00
_____SUCCESS AT THE HARNESS RACES *Barry Meadow*	3.00
_____WINNING AT THE HARNESS RACES—An Expert's Guide *Nick Cammarano*	3.00

HUMOR

_____HOW TO BE A COMEDIAN FOR FUN & PROFIT *King & Laufer*	2.00
_____HOW TO FLATTEN YOUR TUSH *Coach Marge Reardon*	2.00
_____JOKE TELLER'S HANDBOOK *Bob Orben*	3.00
_____JOKES FOR ALL OCCASIONS *Al Schock*	3.00
_____2000 NEW LAUGHS FOR SPEAKERS *Bob Orben*	3.00

HYPNOTISM

_____ADVANCED TECHNIQUES OF HYPNOSIS *Melvin Powers*	2.00
_____BRAINWASHING AND THE CULTS *Paul A. Verdier, Ph.D.*	3.00
_____CHILDBIRTH WITH HYPNOSIS *William S. Kroger, M.D.*	3.00
_____HOW TO SOLVE Your Sex Problems with Self-Hypnosis *Frank S. Caprio, M.D.*	3.00
_____HOW TO STOP SMOKING THRU SELF-HYPNOSIS *Leslie M. LeCron*	3.00
_____HOW TO USE AUTO-SUGGESTION EFFECTIVELY *John Duckworth*	3.00
_____HOW YOU CAN BOWL BETTER USING SELF-HYPNOSIS *Jack Heise*	3.00
_____HOW YOU CAN PLAY BETTER GOLF USING SELF-HYPNOSIS *Jack Heise*	2.00
_____HYPNOSIS AND SELF-HYPNOSIS *Bernard Hollander, M.D.*	3.00
_____HYPNOTISM *(Originally published in 1893) Carl Sextus*	3.00
_____HYPNOTISM & PSYCHIC PHENOMENA *Simeon Edmunds*	3.00
_____HYPNOTISM MADE EASY *Dr. Ralph Winn*	3.00
_____HYPNOTISM MADE PRACTICAL *Louis Orton*	3.00
_____HYPNOTISM REVEALED *Melvin Powers*	2.00
_____HYPNOTISM TODAY *Leslie LeCron and Jean Bordeaux, Ph.D.*	4.00
_____MODERN HYPNOSIS *Lesley Kuhn & Salvatore Russo, Ph.D.*	5.00
_____NEW CONCEPTS OF HYPNOSIS *Bernard C. Gindes, M.D.*	4.00
_____NEW SELF-HYPNOSIS *Paul Adams*	3.00
_____POST-HYPNOTIC INSTRUCTIONS—Suggestions for Therapy *Arnold Furst*	3.00
_____PRACTICAL GUIDE TO SELF-HYPNOSIS *Melvin Powers*	3.00
_____PRACTICAL HYPNOTISM *Philip Magonet, M.D.*	2.00
_____SECRETS OF HYPNOTISM *S. J. Van Pelt, M.D.*	3.00
_____SELF-HYPNOSIS A Conditioned-Response Technique *Laurance Sparks*	4.00
_____SELF-HYPNOSIS Its Theory, Technique & Application *Melvin Powers*	3.00
_____THERAPY THROUGH HYPNOSIS *edited by Raphael H. Rhodes*	4.00

JUDAICA

_____HOW TO LIVE A RICHER & FULLER LIFE *Rabbi Edgar F. Magnin*	2.00
_____MODERN ISRAEL *Lily Edelman*	2.00
_____ROMANCE OF HASSIDISM *Jacob S. Minkin*	2.50
_____SERVICE OF THE HEART *Evelyn Garfiel, Ph.D.*	4.00
_____STORY OF ISRAEL IN COINS *Jean & Maurice Gould*	2.00
_____STORY OF ISRAEL IN STAMPS *Maxim & Gabriel Shamir*	1.00
_____TREASURY OF COMFORT *edited by Rabbi Sidney Greenberg*	4.00

JUST FOR WOMEN

_____COSMOPOLITAN'S GUIDE TO MARVELOUS MEN Fwd. by *Helen Gurley Brown*	3.00
_____COSMOPOLITAN'S HANG-UP HANDBOOK Foreword by *Helen Gurley Brown*	4.00
_____COSMOPOLITAN'S LOVE BOOK—A Guide to Ecstasy in Bed	3.00
_____COSMOPOLITAN'S NEW ETIQUETTE GUIDE Fwd. by *Helen Gurley Brown*	4.00
_____I AM A COMPLEAT WOMAN *Doris Hagopian & Karen O'Connor Sweeney*	3.00
_____JUST FOR WOMEN—A Guide to the Female Body *Richard E. Sand, M.D.*	4.00
_____NEW APPROACHES TO SEX IN MARRIAGE *John E. Eichenlaub, M.D.*	3.00
_____SEXUALLY ADEQUATE FEMALE *Frank S. Caprio, M.D.*	3.00
_____YOUR FIRST YEAR OF MARRIAGE *Dr. Tom McGinnis*	3.00

MARRIAGE, SEX & PARENTHOOD

_____ABILITY TO LOVE *Dr. Allan Fromme*	5.00
_____ENCYCLOPEDIA OF MODERN SEX & LOVE TECHNIQUES *Macandrew*	4.00
_____GUIDE TO SUCCESSFUL MARRIAGE *Drs. Albert Ellis & Robert Harper*	4.00
_____HOW TO RAISE AN EMOTIONALLY HEALTHY, HAPPY CHILD *A. Ellis*	3.00
_____IMPOTENCE & FRIGIDITY *Edwin W. Hirsch, M.D.*	3.00
_____SEX WITHOUT GUILT *Albert Ellis, Ph.D.*	3.00
_____SEXUALLY ADEQUATE MALE *Frank S. Caprio, M.D.*	3.00

MELVIN POWERS' MAIL ORDER LIBRARY

____HOW TO GET RICH IN MAIL ORDER *Melvin Powers*	15.00
____HOW TO WRITE A GOOD ADVERTISEMENT *Victor O. Schwab*	15.00
____WORLD WIDE MAIL ORDER SHOPPER'S GUIDE *Eugene V. Moller*	5.00

METAPHYSICS & OCCULT

____BOOK OF TALISMANS, AMULETS & ZODIACAL GEMS *William Pavitt*	4.00
____CONCENTRATION—A Guide to Mental Mastery *Mouni Sadhu*	3.00
____CRITIQUES OF GOD *Edited by Peter Angeles*	7.00
____DREAMS & OMENS REVEALED *Fred Gettings*	3.00
____EXTRASENSORY PERCEPTION *Simeon Edmunds*	2.00
____EXTRA-TERRESTRIAL INTELLIGENCE—The First Encounter	6.00
____FORTUNE TELLING WITH CARDS *P. Foli*	3.00
____HANDWRITING ANALYSIS MADE EASY *John Marley*	3.00
____HANDWRITING TELLS *Nadya Olyanova*	5.00
____HOW TO UNDERSTAND YOUR DREAMS *Geoffrey A. Dudley*	3.00
____ILLUSTRATED YOGA *William Zorn*	3.00
____IN DAYS OF GREAT PEACE *Mouni Sadhu*	3.00
____KING SOLOMON'S TEMPLE IN THE MASONIC TRADITION *Alex Horne*	5.00
____LSD—THE AGE OF MIND *Bernard Roseman*	2.00
____MAGICIAN—His training and work *W. E. Butler*	3.00
____MEDITATION *Mouni Sadhu*	4.00
____MODERN NUMEROLOGY *Morris C. Goodman*	3.00
____NUMEROLOGY—ITS FACTS AND SECRETS *Ariel Yvon Taylor*	3.00
____NUMEROLOGY MADE EASY *W. Mykian*	3.00
____PALMISTRY MADE EASY *Fred Gettings*	3.00
____PALMISTRY MADE PRACTICAL *Elizabeth Daniels Squire*	3.00
____PALMISTRY SECRETS REVEALED *Henry Frith*	3.00
____PRACTICAL YOGA *Ernest Wood*	3.00
____PROPHECY IN OUR TIME *Martin Ebon*	2.50
____PSYCHOLOGY OF HANDWRITING *Nadya Olyanova*	3.00
____SUPERSTITION—Are you superstitious? *Eric Maple*	2.00
____TAROT *Mouni Sadhu*	5.00
____TAROT OF THE BOHEMIANS *Papus*	5.00
____TEST YOUR ESP *Martin Ebon*	2.00
____WAYS TO SELF-REALIZATION *Mouni Sadhu*	3.00
____WHAT YOUR HANDWRITING REVEALS *Albert E. Hughes*	2.00
____WITCHCRAFT, MAGIC & OCCULTISM—A Fascinating History *W. B. Crow*	5.00
____WITCHCRAFT—THE SIXTH SENSE *Justine Glass*	3.00
____WORLD OF PSYCHIC RESEARCH *Hereward Carrington*	2.00
____YOU CAN ANALYZE HANDWRITING *Robert Holder*	2.00

SELF-HELP & INSPIRATIONAL

____CYBERNETICS WITHIN US *Y. Saparina*	3.00
____DAILY POWER FOR JOYFUL LIVING *Dr. Donald Curtis*	3.00
____DOCTOR PSYCHO-CYBERNETICS *Maxwell Maltz, M.D.*	3.00
____DYNAMIC THINKING *Melvin Powers*	2.00
____EXUBERANCE—Your Guide to Happiness & Fulfillment *Dr. Paul Kurtz*	3.00
____GREATEST POWER IN THE UNIVERSE *U. S. Andersen*	4.00
____GROW RICH WHILE YOU SLEEP *Ben Sweetland*	3.00
____GROWTH THROUGH REASON *Albert Ellis, Ph.D.*	4.00
____GUIDE TO DEVELOPING YOUR POTENTIAL *Herbert A. Otto, Ph.D.*	3.00
____GUIDE TO LIVING IN BALANCE *Frank S. Caprio, M.D.*	2.00
____HELPING YOURSELF WITH APPLIED PSYCHOLOGY *R. Henderson*	2.00
____HELPING YOURSELF WITH PSYCHIATRY *Frank S. Caprio, M.D.*	2.00
____HOW TO ATTRACT GOOD LUCK *A. H. Z. Carr*	3.00
____HOW TO CONTROL YOUR DESTINY *Norvell*	3.00
____HOW TO DEVELOP A WINNING PERSONALITY *Martin Panzer*	3.00
____HOW TO DEVELOP AN EXCEPTIONAL MEMORY *Young & Gibson*	4.00
____HOW TO OVERCOME YOUR FEARS *M. P. Leahy, M.D.*	3.00
____HOW YOU CAN HAVE CONFIDENCE AND POWER *Les Giblin*	3.00
____HUMAN PROBLEMS & HOW TO SOLVE THEM *Dr. Donald Curtis*	3.00
____I CAN *Ben Sweetland*	4.00
____I WILL *Ben Sweetland*	3.00
____LEFT-HANDED PEOPLE *Michael Barsley*	4.00

____MAGIC IN YOUR MIND *U. S. Andersen*	4.00
____MAGIC OF THINKING BIG *Dr. David J. Schwartz*	3.00
____MAGIC POWER OF YOUR MIND *Walter M. Germain*	4.00
____MENTAL POWER THROUGH SLEEP SUGGESTION *Melvin Powers*	2.00
____NEW GUIDE TO RATIONAL LIVING *Albert Ellis, Ph.D. & R. Harper, Ph.D.*	3.00
____OUR TROUBLED SELVES *Dr. Allan Fromme*	3.00
____PSYCHO-CYBERNETICS *Maxwell Maltz, M.D.*	2.00
____SCIENCE OF MIND IN DAILY LIVING *Dr. Donald Curtis*	3.00
____SECRET OF SECRETS *U. S. Andersen*	4.00
____SECRET POWER OF THE PYRAMIDS *U. S. Andersen*	4.00
____STUTTERING AND WHAT YOU CAN DO ABOUT IT *W. Johnson, Ph.D.*	2.50
____SUCCESS-CYBERNETICS *U. S. Andersen*	4.00
____10 DAYS TO A GREAT NEW LIFE *William E. Edwards*	3.00
____THINK AND GROW RICH *Napoleon Hill*	3.00
____THREE MAGIC WORDS *U. S. Andersen*	4.00
____TREASURY OF THE ART OF LIVING *Sidney S. Greenberg*	5.00
____YOU ARE NOT THE TARGET *Laura Huxley*	3.00
____YOUR SUBCONSCIOUS POWER *Charles M. Simmons*	4.00
____YOUR THOUGHTS CAN CHANGE YOUR LIFE *Dr. Donald Curtis*	3.00

SPORTS

____ARCHERY—An Expert's Guide *Dan Stamp*	2.00
____BICYCLING FOR FUN AND GOOD HEALTH *Kenneth E. Luther*	2.00
____BILLIARDS—Pocket • Carom • Three Cushion *Clive Cottingham, Jr.*	3.00
____CAMPING-OUT 101 Ideas & Activities *Bruno Knobel*	2.00
____COMPLETE GUIDE TO FISHING *Vlad Evanoff*	2.00
____HOW TO IMPROVE YOUR RACQUETBALL *Lubarsky, Kaufman, & Scagnetti*	3.00
____HOW TO WIN AT POCKET BILLIARDS *Edward D. Knuchell*	3.00
____JOY OF WALKING *Jack Scagnetti*	3.00
____LEARNING & TEACHING SOCCER SKILLS *Eric Worthington*	3.00
____MOTORCYCLING FOR BEGINNERS *I. G. Edmonds*	3.00
____RACQUETBALL MADE EASY *Steve Lubarsky, Rod Delson & Jack Scagnetti*	3.00
____SECRET OF BOWLING STRIKES *Dawson Taylor*	3.00
____SECRET OF PERFECT PUTTING *Horton Smith & Dawson Taylor*	3.00
____SOCCER—The game & how to play it *Gary Rosenthal*	3.00
____STARTING SOCCER *Edward F. Dolan, Jr.*	2.00
____TABLE TENNIS MADE EASY *Johnny Leach*	2.00

TENNIS LOVERS' LIBRARY

____BEGINNER'S GUIDE TO WINNING TENNIS *Helen Hull Jacobs*	2.00
____HOW TO BEAT BETTER TENNIS PLAYERS *Loring Fiske*	4.00
____HOW TO IMPROVE YOUR TENNIS—Style, Strategy & Analysis *C. Wilson*	2.00
____INSIDE TENNIS—Techniques of Winning *Jim Leighton*	3.00
____PLAY TENNIS WITH ROSEWALL *Ken Rosewall*	2.00
____PSYCH YOURSELF TO BETTER TENNIS *Dr. Walter A. Luszki*	2.00
____SUCCESSFUL TENNIS *Neale Fraser*	2.00
____TENNIS FOR BEGINNERS *Dr. H. A. Murray*	2.00
____TENNIS MADE EASY *Joel Brecheen*	2.00
____WEEKEND TENNIS—How to have fun & win at the same time *Bill Talbert*	3.00
____WINNING WITH PERCENTAGE TENNIS—Smart Strategy *Jack Lowe*	2.00

WILSHIRE PET LIBRARY

____DOG OBEDIENCE TRAINING *Gust Kessopulos*	3.00
____DOG TRAINING MADE EASY & FUN *John W. Kellogg*	3.00
____HOW TO BRING UP YOUR PET DOG *Kurt Unkelbach*	2.00
____HOW TO RAISE & TRAIN YOUR PUPPY *Jeff Griffen*	2.00
____PIGEONS: HOW TO RAISE & TRAIN THEM *William H. Allen, Jr.*	2.00

The books listed above can be obtained from your book dealer or directly from Melvin Powers. When ordering, please remit 50¢ per book postage & handling. Send for our free illustrated catalog of self-improvement books.

Melvin Powers

12015 Sherman Road, No. Hollywood, California 91605

WILSHIRE HORSE LOVERS' LIBRARY

____AMATEUR HORSE BREEDER *A. C. Leighton Hardman*	3.00
____AMERICAN QUARTER HORSE IN PICTURES *Margaret Cabell Self*	3.00
____APPALOOSA HORSE *Donna & Bill Richardson*	3.00
____ARABIAN HORSE *Reginald S. Summerhays*	2.00
____ART OF WESTERN RIDING *Suzanne Norton Jones*	3.00
____AT THE HORSE SHOW *Margaret Cabell Self*	3.00
____BACK-YARD FOAL *Peggy Jett Pittinger*	3.00
____BACK-YARD HORSE *Peggy Jett Pittinger*	3.00
____BASIC DRESSAGE *Jean Froissard*	2.00
____BEGINNER'S GUIDE TO HORSEBACK RIDING *Sheila Wall*	2.00
____BEGINNER'S GUIDE TO THE WESTERN HORSE *Natlee Kenoyer*	2.00
____BITS—THEIR HISTORY, USE AND MISUSE *Louis Taylor*	3.00
____BREAKING & TRAINING THE DRIVING HORSE *Doris Ganton*	2.00
____BREAKING YOUR HORSE'S BAD HABITS *W. Dayton Sumner*	3.00
____CAVALRY MANUAL OF HORSEMANSHIP *Gordon Wright*	3.00
____COMPLETE TRAINING OF HORSE AND RIDER *Colonel Alois Podhajsky*	4.00
____DISORDERS OF THE HORSE & WHAT TO DO ABOUT THEM *E. Hanauer*	3.00
____DOG TRAINING MADE EASY & FUN *John W. Kellogg*	3.00
____DRESSAGE—A Study of the Finer Points in Riding *Henry Wynmalen*	4.00
____DRIVING HORSES *Sallie Walrond*	3.00
____ENDURANCE RIDING *Ann Hyland*	2.00
____EQUITATION *Jean Froissard*	4.00
____FIRST AID FOR HORSES *Dr. Charles H. Denning, Jr.*	2.00
____FUN OF RAISING A COLT *Rubye & Frank Griffith*	3.00
____FUN ON HORSEBACK *Margaret Cabell Self*	4.00
____GYMKHANA GAMES *Natlee Kenoyer*	2.00
____HORSE DISEASES—Causes, Symptoms & Treatment *Dr. H. G. Belschner*	4.00
____HORSE OWNER'S CONCISE GUIDE *Elsie V. Hanauer*	2.00
____HORSE SELECTION & CARE FOR BEGINNERS *George H. Conn*	3.00
____HORSE SENSE—A complete guide to riding and care *Alan Deacon*	4.00
____HORSEBACK RIDING FOR BEGINNERS *Louis Taylor*	4.00
____HORSEBACK RIDING MADE EASY & FUN *Sue Henderson Coen*	3.00
____HORSES—Their Selection, Care & Handling *Margaret Cabell Self*	3.00
____HOW TO BUY A BETTER HORSE & SELL THE HORSE YOU OWN	3.00
____HOW TO ENJOY YOUR QUARTER HORSE *Williard H. Porter*	3.00
____HUNTER IN PICTURES *Margaret Cabell Self*	2.00
____ILLUSTRATED BOOK OF THE HORSE *S. Sidney* (8½" x 11")	10.00
____ILLUSTRATED HORSE MANAGEMENT—400 Illustrations *Dr. E. Mayhew*	6.00
____ILLUSTRATED HORSE TRAINING *Captain M. H. Hayes*	5.00
____ILLUSTRATED HORSEBACK RIDING FOR BEGINNERS *Jeanne Mellin*	2.00
____JUMPING—Learning & Teaching *Jean Froissard*	3.00
____KNOW ALL ABOUT HORSES *Harry Disston*	3.00
____LAME HORSE—Causes, Symptoms & Treatment *Dr. James R. Rooney*	4.00
____LAW & YOUR HORSE *Edward H. Greene*	5.00
____LIPIZZANERS & THE SPANISH RIDING SCHOOL *W. Reuter* (4¼" x 6")	2.50
____MANUAL OF HORSEMANSHIP *Harold Black*	5.00
____MORGAN HORSE IN PICTURES *Margaret Cabell Self*	2.00
____MOVIE HORSES—The Fascinating Techniques of Training *Anthony Amaral*	2.00
____POLICE HORSES *Judith Campbell*	2.00
____PRACTICAL GUIDE TO HORSESHOEING	3.00
____PRACTICAL GUIDE TO OWNING YOUR OWN HORSE *Steven D. Price*	2.00
____PRACTICAL HORSE PSYCHOLOGY *Moyra Williams*	3.00
____PROBLEM HORSES Guide for Curing Serious Behavior Habits *Summerhays*	2.00
____REINSMAN OF THE WEST—BRIDLES & BITS *Ed Connell*	4.00
____RESCHOOLING THE THOROUGHBRED *Peggy Jett Pittenger*	3.00
____RIDE WESTERN *Louis Taylor*	3.00
____SCHOOLING YOUR YOUNG HORSE *George Wheatley*	2.00
____STABLE MANAGEMENT FOR THE OWNER-GROOM *George Wheatley*	4.00
____STALLION MANAGEMENT—A Guide for Stud Owners *A. C. Hardman*	3.00
____TEACHING YOUR HORSE TO JUMP *W. J. Froud*	2.00
____TRAIL HORSES & TRAIL RIDING *Anne & Perry Westbrook*	2.00
____TRAINING YOUR HORSE TO SHOW *Neale Haley*	3.00
____TREATING COMMON DISEASES OF YOUR HORSE *Dr. George H. Conn*	3.00
____TREATING HORSE AILMENTS *G. W. Serth*	2.00
____WESTERN HORSEBACK RIDING *Glen Balch*	3.00
____YOU AND YOUR PONY *Pepper Mainwaring Healey* (8½" x 11")	6.00
____YOUR FIRST HORSE *George C. Saunders, M.D.*	3.00
____YOUR PONY BOOK *Hermann Wiederhold*	2.00
____YOUR WESTERN HORSE *Nelson C. Nye*	2.00

*The books listed above can be obtained from your book dealer or directly from
Melvin Powers. When ordering, please remit 50¢ per book postage & handling.
Send for our free illustrated catalog of self-improvement books.*

Melvin Powers

12015 Sherman Road, No. Hollywood, California 91605

NOTES